THE KIWI
MAN
CAVE
Manual

THE KIWI MAN CAVE Manual

STEVE HALE

Bateman

Published in 2016 by David Bateman Ltd
30 Tarndale Grove, Albany, Auckland, New Zealand

www.batemanpublishing.co.nz

ISBN 978-1-86953-946-7

Book design: Cheryl Smith
Printed in China by Asia Pacific Offset

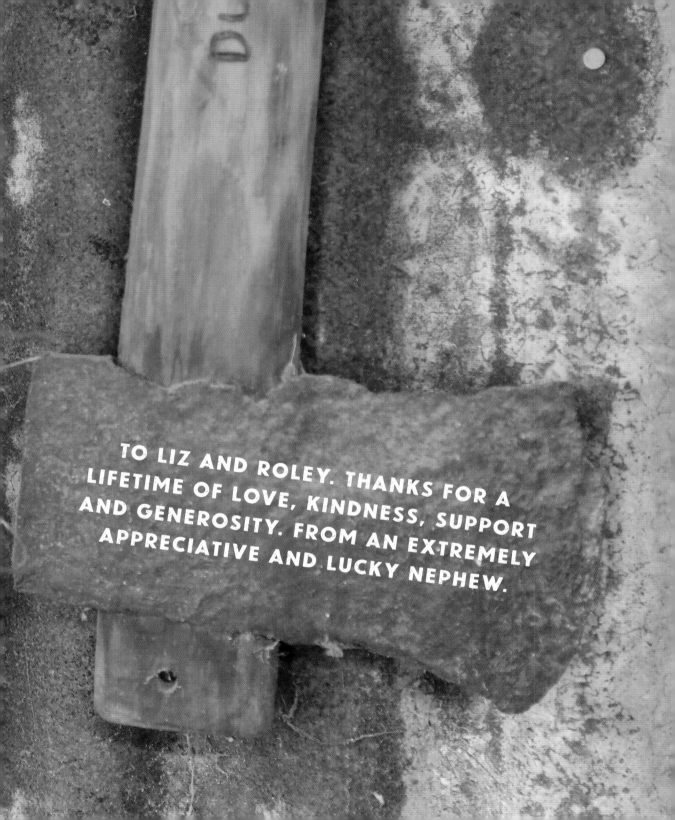

CONTENTS

FOREWORD

No one's really talking about it. While headlines are preoccupied with the housing crisis, I guess that means we could be in the midst of a Man Cave crisis, too. It's hard to get statistics on this, but, given that young men are finding it harder to own their own home, then their chances of having a Man Cave are also diminishing.

But men have withstood other crises before. Remember Leaky Cave Syndrome? Several Man Caves were found to be damp, poorly weatherproofed, poorly insulated, poorly everything really. But did you see men complaining about their leaky caves on national TV or in the *Herald*? No. They just suffered in silence. Some of them simply sold the pool table and moved on. Others, as a last resort, even contemplated using the tools inside the cave to remedy the situation, before moving on.

Leaky Cave Syndrome is nothing new of course. That's been around for centuries. Those who suffered in the early years were victims of the very first trickle-down effect. That's why, if you lived in one of many caves in a mountain face, you'd want the penthouse cave. Nothing much has changed really.

Since then, Man Caves have helped shape history.

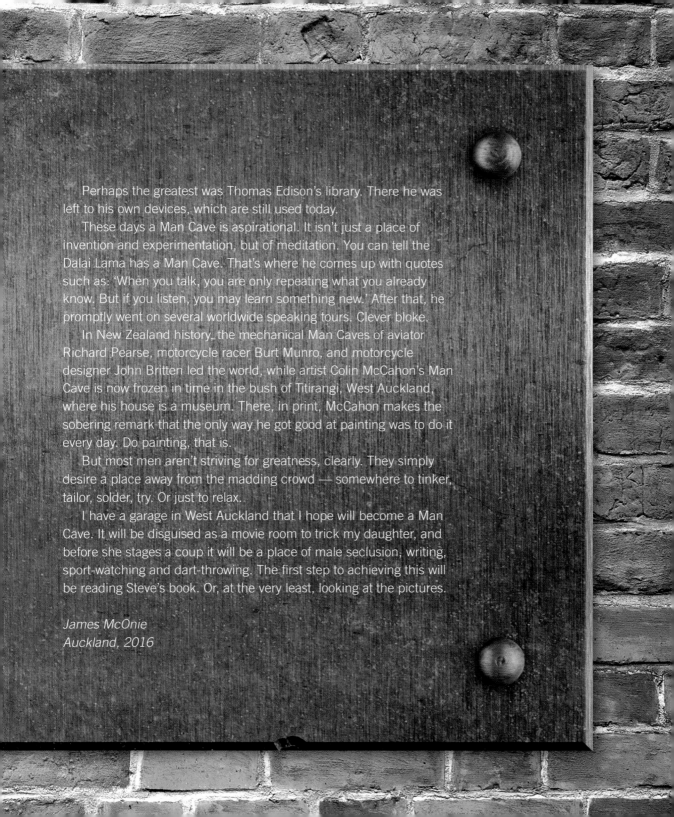

Perhaps the greatest was Thomas Edison's library. There he was left to his own devices, which are still used today.

These days a Man Cave is aspirational. It isn't just a place of invention and experimentation, but of meditation. You can tell the Dalai Lama has a Man Cave. That's where he comes up with quotes such as: 'When you talk, you are only repeating what you already know. But if you listen, you may learn something new.' After that, he promptly went on several worldwide speaking tours. Clever bloke.

In New Zealand history, the mechanical Man Caves of aviator Richard Pearse, motorcycle racer Burt Munro, and motorcycle designer John Britten led the world, while artist Colin McCahon's Man Cave is now frozen in time in the bush of Titirangi, West Auckland, where his house is a museum. There, in print, McCahon makes the sobering remark that the only way he got good at painting was to do it every day. Do painting, that is.

But most men aren't striving for greatness, clearly. They simply desire a place away from the madding crowd — somewhere to tinker, tailor, solder, try. Or just to relax.

I have a garage in West Auckland that I hope will become a Man Cave. It will be disguised as a movie room to trick my daughter, and before she stages a coup it will be a place of male seclusion, writing, sport-watching and dart-throwing. The first step to achieving this will be reading Steve's book. Or, at the very least, looking at the pictures.

James McOnie
Auckland, 2016

Aaron

THE MINE'S BIGGER THAN YOURS FISHING CLUB

'I like three things: rugby, fishing, beer … and a bit of cricket,' beams Aaron, whose self-built Man Cave is a shrine to his three — make that four — passions in life.

'It all started with a fridge,' he explains, 'eight years ago actually, which I bought on Trade Me.' As far as purpose-built suburban Man Caves go, Aaron's effort — which includes a well-stocked commercial beer fridge, a pool table, a fish-smoker and a 55-inch tele — well, this pad takes some beating. 'The TV in here is bigger than the other three in the house,' he laughs.

'This room is actually marked down as a workshop on the house plans. The front window was designed to be removed so a sectional door can be installed, giving the option of an extra garage. But what bloke wouldn't want a Man Cave?'

One thing our host openly admits he will do differently when building his next Man Cave (and adjoining home) is the bathroom's layout. Currently the sink can only be accessed when the door is shut. It's a surprising design flaw considering Aaron is a master builder by trade, although to be fair even subtle imperfections can be found in the works of Van Gogh, Michelangelo, Rembrandt and Picasso.

Aaron's pad also doubles as headquarters for the Mine's Bigger Than Yours Fishing Club. 'You have to weigh in a fish every six months or you owe the club a box of beer. It costs $55 to join, 50 of that goes towards prizes for the first, second and third heaviest fish. The remaining five bucks is spent on a bit of steak for the barbeque. We have around 30 members, and most manage to weigh in a fish each season.'

Right on cue, two meaty snapper which had been smoking away nearby are plonked on the bar for our evening meal. Both were caught the previous weekend while Aaron was competing in the Dr Fish competition, an annual event between local rugby clubs Waihou and Cobras.

One of Aaron's cats has been named after his beloved Waihou club, and the fulsome feline has provided two rather unusual artefacts, which are on display by the bar for all to see. One specimen jar contains Waihou's testicles, while another houses a rather large piece of soft bait, which the cat swallowed prior to having it extracted by a local vet.

Just like the cat's crown jewels, many other treasures on display come with an engaging explanation. The American flag, for example, was bought from a flea market held directly in front of the World Trade Center on 10 September 2001, less than 24 hours before the buildings were destroyed by terrorists.

The large inflatable bottle of Gosling's rum was illegally procured by Aaron from a police tent during the Bermuda World Classic Sevens Tournament he attended. 'I managed to fully deflate it and get away without being apprehended,' he laughs. The striking 2011 Rugby World Cup billboard was prised away from the Te Atatu Peninsula RSA. Aaron enlisted the services of local sign-writer Peter Stanish to add fulltime scores for every pool and knockout match played.

A complete box-set of official match programmes from the 2011 Rugby World Cup is on display, as well as scarves and programmes from the knockout matches he attended at the 2015 tournament. In addition, Aaron has an impressive collection of international rugby and cricket programmes dating back to the 1960s. One item, in particular, a programme from the infamously abandoned South Africa versus Waikato game in 1981, personally hand-signed by the entire Springbok touring party, is extremely rare and highly collectable.

The 2011 All Black jersey signed by both winning coach Graham Henry and replacement first-five Stephen Donald would have to rank as one of the most iconic,

distinctly Kiwi Mantiques I have encountered throughout my travels. 'Initially, Ted [Graham Henry] signed the jersey for me, but I didn't get Beaver's [Donald's] signature until years later at the 2015 Rugby World Cup when he flew over to join our tour party.'

Aaron enjoyed an eventful time en route to that tournament, being hospitalised in Bangkok. In the best traditions of heroic All Black skipper Richie McCaw, whose pain tolerance is second to none, Aaron refused to be sidelined by any medical condition. 'I still had a drip in my arm the day before the All Blacks played France in Cardiff, but there was no way in Hell I was going to miss that game.'

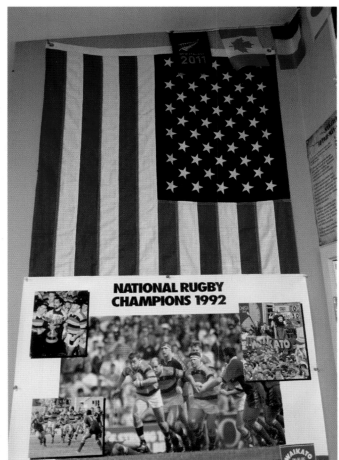

NATIONAL RUGBY CHAMPIONS 1992

Man Cave! No Wife ~ No Kids ~ No Problems!

Steve

THE APACHE
INN

'When I was a kid — you know when you played cowboys and Indians? — well, I was always the Indian,' recalls Steve, proprietor of The Apache Inn. 'And I also used to love watching programmes like *F Troop* and *The High Chaparral*.

'I've always found Indians fascinating. When I got older I started having them put on my arms,' says the heavily tattooed Kapiti Coast resident. 'I love American Indian history.'

He admits that travelling to the United States to set foot on the sacred ground where The Battle of Little Big Horn was fought, or to Lone Pine where Sitting Bull was killed, is at the top of his bucket list.

'It's just a small space in here. I wanted to keep it this size intentionally. There's no TV, so you actually have to talk to each other,' he explains. 'We use it a lot. We've

had up to 20 people in here.' Steve plans to extend The Apache by adding an adjoining deck to make the most of the Paraparaumu sunshine.

'My brother had a bar in Aussie called The Saw Miller's Arms, and that gave me the bug. I wanted my own space and I needed a theme. I didn't want to do rugby, and with my love of Indians it sort of took off from there.

'My brother sent me over a few pieces, then I started scouring antique stores and Trade Me. People now drop Indian things off to my wife at the chemist's for my bar.

'That's my pride,' beams Steve, pointing to a wooden carving. 'Geronimo. Twenty bucks off Trade Me. You can't complain about that. My wife's always asking what I've bought now. But I can't stop.

'It's exciting, too,' remarks Steve, referring to collecting. 'I go to antique shops just looking for little knick-knacks. My son Dane was in Chicago and sent me a Blackhawks ice hockey puck. I love stuff like that.

'I bought the beer tap and barrel off Trade Me, about seven years ago. It came from the old Wairoa Public Bar. I don't have it hooked up; it's just a novelty thing. The bar was actually my mother-in-law's. She's passed away now, but she gave this bar a fair bit of use in her day. I gave it a sand and paint, and decided to keep it in her memory.

'The old man and I boxed off this area and lined it. It was too small to be a car garage. I was going to put a ranch slider at the front to open it up, but the tilt door works okay. There's always little things to do.

'We had the World Cup trophy in here last year. I was at work, but my son [All Blacks hooker Dane Coles] texted me to say that he had the cup with him. It was short notice, but we rounded up the family and rushed home. That was bloody special.'

Tucked away in another small space, connected to The Apache Inn by an internal door, is a tiny rugby museum. Steve has meticulously presented an impressive assortment of memorabilia, which includes a shrine to his favourite All Black team, the 1970 side that toured South Africa. 'I come out here quite a lot, just to chill out. I clean stuff, and rearrange it. I always find things I forget I had.'

Steve has installed a rather formidable security system to guard his beloved assets: two loyal bulldogs who ensure that all possessions remain on-site. The Apache Inn is in safe hands.

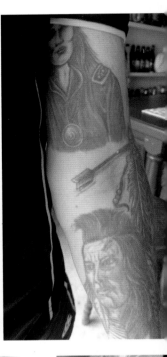

The Peggy's Collection

Craig

CAPTAIN
HURRICANE

'Just as many people know me as "Captain Hurricane" as by my first name,' admits Craig. 'I come out to the farm once or twice a week to see Mum and Dad for tea. I usually pop out here to Hurricanes HQ and reminisce. Sometimes I have a quiet beer.

'The old family homestead is on this farm. Dad and his four brothers actually used to live in here, growing up many years ago,' says Craig, standing in his shrine. 'I moved out here when I was 16. Used to have the boys out here and enjoy a few quiets. Turn the stereo up loud and have a bit of fun.

'When I first moved out here I painted the walls pink; don't really know what I was thinking. Then the posters started going up. Originally, I only had half the space for myself, and my parents' camping gear filled the remainder. I've had the whole shed full for about 12 years now. I'm looking at getting a shipping container and expanding. As you can see, there's no more space. I had a few of the Canes players in here for a visit a few seasons ago: Tony Penn and Paul Tito. They both loved the place.'

Hurricane-inspired street signs, full-sized cardboard cut-outs of star players, collections of rugby balls, ties, jerseys and figurines engulf the space, while the *pièce de résistance* has to be the single bed draped in Hurricanes linen. 'I got the street signs made up last season. I already had some of the road signs. Adelaide Road was where the old Athletic Park in Wellington used to be.

'Not much sun gets in here. So some of these pictures are 18 to 20 years old, and they're still in really good nick.'

I made mention of an action photo on the wall of giant Hurricanes prop Billy Cavubati. 'He's gone back to bouncing now: I saw him when I was at the races in Wellington, and was trying to remember how I knew him. Had a yarn with Bill. He's still a unit,' laughs Craig.

The walls, floor and some parts of the ceiling are decorated with an incredible assortment of Hurricanes and Wellington rugby memorabilia. 'I live in the Taranaki, but Wellington has always been the team I support. I have received more than my share of grief about that over the years,' says the Hawera dairy farmer. 'Taranaki are my second favourite team, though.

'To be fair, in 1996 when Super 12 rugby kicked off, I didn't really know much about the Hurricanes. I went to their game up in New Plymouth. The next season I really started getting into it.' Craig has a set of tickets from the first-ever Super 12 match, which also doubled as the inaugural game of professional rugby played in New Zealand; Hurricanes versus Blues at Palmerston North, 1 March 1996. 'My old man went to it. Shit, mate, it's hard to remember where everything is these days … Here they are,' he says finally, after scouring the room for nearly a minute. Craig directs me to a small frame hanging next to the bed. 'It was a close game in the end,' he recalls. 'The Blues scored all the tries, but the Canes kept in the hunt by slotting penalties.

'Farming does limit when I can get away,' says the affable sharemilker, 'but I still try to attend as many games as I can.' Being the Hurricanes' most recognisable supporter has seen Craig receive his fair share of media attention. An array of published articles written about him are on display in another corner. 'I've even been on the *Holmes* show,' he grins. 'They took me up to New Plymouth in 2005, before the Canes played the Sharks, and chucked me in the Captain Hurricane suit for the afternoon.'

Tana Umaga is Craig's favourite Hurricanes player of all time, with Christian Cullen a close second. A striking, impressive carving of Umaga, Cullen and Lomu rests in a glass display case. 'A joker from the Hawke's Bay who is a carver saw me on the *Holmes* show and got in touch with me. This is a one-off piece he did. Handmade, really fine detail. That was worth three and a half grand 12 years ago. I'm pretty rapt to have that; it would have to be my pride and joy.'

Craig has collected every single Hurricanes playing jersey ever produced. He was even invited to attend the 2016 official adidas jersey launch in Auckland, a testament to his undying loyalty. He has framed a few jerseys, but the majority hang on racks or are neatly folded away, only to be brought out for special occasions. 'Four hundred bucks is a lot to frame a jersey. I know there's a lot of glass in it, but it's still a lot of money.'

Craig happily hangs his burgeoning Canes jersey collection on the washing-line to pose in front of for a photograph. After it is suggested that he is quite photogenic, the big fella cheerfully replies, 'You've got to look your best, don't you? After all, this publication is quite likely to be read all over the world.'

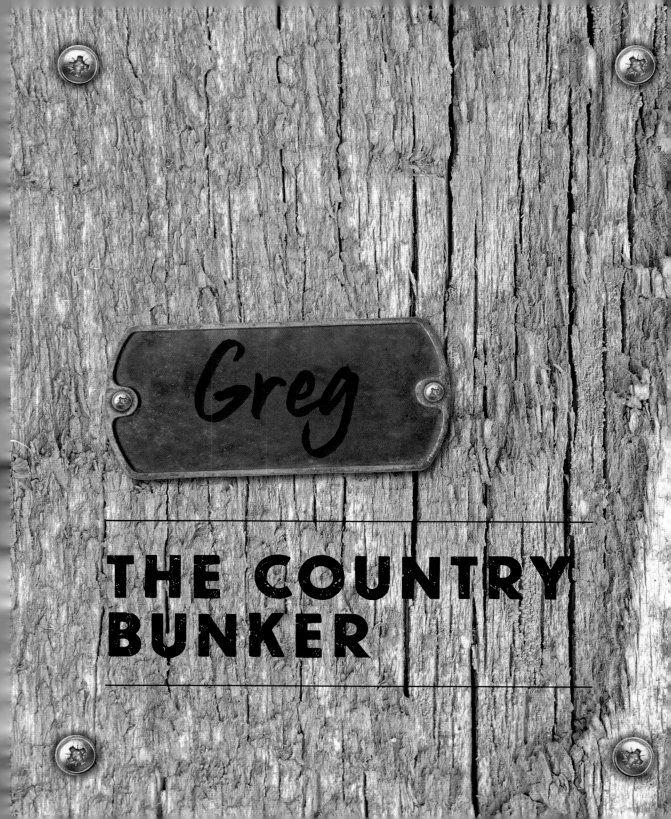

Greg

THE COUNTRY BUNKER

Greg has created his own slice of Heaven, located less than 3 metres from the front door of his house, smack-bang in the centre of town. 'I had the space there, a vacant bit of dirt, so I thought, "Why not?"' As a result, the time it takes Greg to mow his lawns has been halved. 'When we bought the place 12 years ago, I planted all the natives, which have evolved and form a nice backdrop to the shed.'

When asked how much use his pad gets, Greg's face sports a huge smile. 'Stephen,' he beams, 'when the weather's good, we sit out there nearly every night. With the late-afternoon summer sun, it's actually too hot to sit on the front deck of our house, but out there under the trees it's cool and peaceful. We light up the barbeque. It's quite amazing, it's just given us that extra space from here. As they say, everybody needs a big deck,' he laughs.

Greg has taken his favourite vices out to his slice of Shangri-La. 'I've got Trackside out there, too; Sky TV to watch the races,' says Greg, who is partial to the odd flutter. He also enjoys a good radio commentary, including crackle and static, listening intently to the old radio, complete with leather carry-case, and fuelled by double-A batteries.

The front door of Greg's bunker was originally a billboard. 'I had it sitting behind the lodge for a while,' he explains, 'so decided to measure it up and put the Skilsaw through it.' The rough-sawn timber panelling interior is offset by an interesting array of curios that Greg has acquired over the years, including a steel-cast toy fire engine, badges from one of his grandfather's cars, a vintage child's scooter, and strings of fake flowers which decorate the ceiling.

Two photos in particular — one of the legendary Phar Lap, and another, a portrait of 'The King' himself, Elvis Presley — represent two of Greg's passions in life. A keen musician, Greg has fronted many bands over the years with his gravelly tones and acumen on the steel strings. 'My father taught me how to play when I was a kid,' reveals Greg, while tuning one of several instruments leaning against the wall, and then plucking an impressive version of 'Dueling Banjos'.

'I had a mate who is on a big sheep station here from Gisborne in the weekend. We were in here watching the rugby on Friday night. It was a better atmosphere than going to the game. He enjoyed himself so much in my shed that he kept saying how he has to get one of these.

'The smaller the space the better, as it's far easier to create character and atmosphere,' says Greg. 'In the old days the pub would close at 10, and then you'd queue up for 50 metres at the bottle store to buy your booze before going to a party in someone's kitchen with 15 people. You can create real energy and ambience with 15 people in a small space. Put 15 people in a hall and it feels dead. Fewer people in a small space. Lots of energy and more fun.'

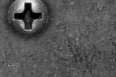

Adrian

HEAVY METAL

'I'm a big believer,' says Adrian, while hammering away at a piece of steel on an enormous anvil, 'in following your passion. Whatever that maybe. If you do that, everything else will come naturally.'

Adrian started out forging twisted wine racks from scrap on the deck at home, working late into the night. Friends and family looked at Adrian's early pieces and wondered if he'd had some sort of trauma injury they hadn't been informed of.

Undeterred, the Te Aroha man continued to dream, design and create. Today, his character-laden workshop and mesmerising scrapyard bear testament to what can be achieved with passion, self-belief and ingenuity.

Adrian's workshop would have to be every bloke's dream. A huge selection of heavy machinery, welding equipment, multiple workspaces and an overhead gantry. Huge framed posters of bands, including Iron Maiden, The Doors and Slipknot, hang on stained plywood walls. Adrian's preferred genre of music ranges from heavy to heavier … As he works, Metal anthems bellow from strategically placed speakers which have been boxed into the walls. The spacious premises ooze natural light.

The heavy-metal sculptor has no time for the gym; he is workshop-strong, having spent a lifetime lugging ridiculously heavy pieces of metal from his yard to the workshop, then wrestling the cumbersome items into workable positions.

Hanging above the office window is one of Adrian's breakthrough creations. 'The Triumph 650 was my first big piece. It took 300 hours to complete. I've learnt a lot from it, though. There are a lot of things I would change if I did it again. My style has developed. For me, it's a reminder of the time that was special in my life. I really wanted to achieve something, and looking at it now reminds me that, whatever work I undertake in the future, I always want to put that same level of effort in. Each piece has to be special: I don't ever want to be in a position where it becomes a chore.

'Mistakes are great,' he admits with refreshing candour. 'I really do welcome them, because they steer me in a different direction. It means next time I can explore them and develop my style.' The growth and magic takes place when new ideas develop mid-flow, often spurred on by human error.

'There have been attempts to replicate my work, but those who copy never last long. They come unstuck because they don't understand exactly what I'm thinking at the time, or what I'm trying to do. They can only keep reproducing one piece, whereas I continue to develop my style and move on. I don't want to keep doing the same thing; my style continually evolves.

'I really struggle to visualise what my work will finally look like, and don't ever want to. I have an idea — I do know which pieces I'm going to use, and can conceptualise how they will fit together — but the overall composition will take different directions. I don't ever want to limit myself by following a rigid plan.'

Adrian has found himself rejecting some lucrative offers from some major players in the entertainment industry simply because he doesn't want to be pigeon-holed into mass-producing his work.

He prefers to work in a clutter-free environment, surrounded by images, themes and textures which resonate with his psyche. 'I don't really think too much about the end product when I'm building. I just pick materials I like and think about styles that I like.'

The office, which is located at the rear of the workshop, feels almost mystical, a deft mix of new and old. Adrian manages to entwine vintage or classical principles

with a grunty contemporary feel. The dark timber shelving, workspaces and exposed rock-work fit symbiotically alongside vintage fire-extinguishers, the old safe, and the step-ladder which glides along a brass rail, providing access to a loud and vibrant music collection. Vintage ladders and an exhaust-pipe hang between rustic exposed beams.

Outside, the collection of Adrian's scrap — hundreds of tonnes' worth, set amongst plantings, stairwells and quirky board-walks — is equally impressive. Old chainsaws, gantry hooks. Ordered meticulously, it serves a dual purpose, primarily to supply Adrian with material for ongoing projects, but the yard has also become a hit with visitors. 'Funnily enough, ladies tend to spend much longer in there than the men. They love it. I think a few wives go home and give their husbands grief about how ordered everything is here in my workshop.' Adrian smiles. 'But I can't have it any other way.'

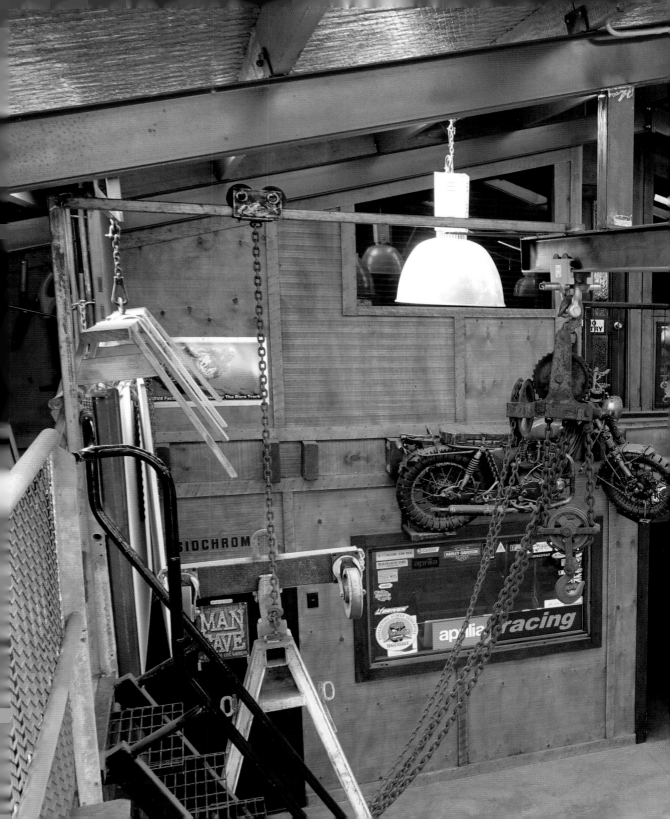

Sir Peter

THE MADNESS
OF SIR PETER

The right honourable Sir Peter Charles Leitch has never been a bloke to do anything by halves. His enormous sporting memorabilia collection is another classic example of New Zealand's favourite butcher's ability to move mountains.

While rugby league features prominently, Sir Peter is quick to point out that he's always been a lover of all sports and has many wonderful mementos on display from some the world's greatest athletes, including Muhammad Ali, Tiger Woods and Rafael Nadal. From tennis to soccer, cricket, basketball, baseball and the Olympics, exhibits from all codes imaginable hang side by side.

'This collection is not just about league. It's for all sports. And it's for the people, too. For example, Sir Graham Henry and I get on very well. I've made so many wonderful friends through being involved with sport. That's what it's really all about, mate.'

Sir Peter's amazing haul began, as all collections do, with a single jersey and a few mementos, before getting out of hand.

'It does help when you're running a business that was going okay and you have a bit of cash up your sleeve,' he admits. 'When I sold my business, I had an empty factory and a couple of containers full of gear. So I opened a sports museum at 23 Holmes Road, Manurewa. My wife told me not to open it, but, being a male, I didn't listen to her.'

Today, his entire collection is on display for the public, fittingly at Mount Smart Stadium, home of his beloved New Zealand Warriors. The NRL club retired its number 19 playing jersey in Sir Peter's honour, testament to his fanatical support of the Auckland-based club since its inception in 1995.

Both stairwells and the entire concourse of the East Stand now house Sir Peter's stunning collection. His involvement with rugby league began in 1971, after he gifted the Mangere East Hawks a few meat-packs to help out with fundraising. He soon became a major sponsor of the club, and a selection of vintage Hawks jerseys with *The Mad Butcher* emblazoned over the torso form a small but heart-warming and fitting part of the Leitch collection.

The move to Mount Smart was a mammoth task; a process Sir Peter reveals was made possible by a wonderful group of people, many of whom volunteered their time and skills. 'The move cost around $100,000 by the time we finished. We had only been here a few months and I learnt the council wanted to shift us and the Warriors out of the joint. That did nothing good for my depression at the time,' he reflects.

'It's not the perfect venue,' he concedes. 'The windows really needed to be tinted, but council wouldn't let us do that. But there's some pretty special stuff in here, and it's far better than looking at bare walls. I wouldn't have a clue with dates, to be fair, mate,' Sir Peter reveals candidly after being asked when he accrued various items.

There are far too many items on display for Sir Peter to list all of his favourites, although several exhibits stand out for sentimental reasons. Like the rectangular framed photo of the 2005 Kiwi squad, which hangs proudly in his lounge, situated in the Colin Kay Upper West grandstand. 'I was the Kiwi manager, and managed the team that beat Australia 24–0 at Leeds in 2005. That's my favourite picture.' A personally signed photo from the immortal Muhammad Ali is another treasured memento.

A boxing glove from the Yellow Ribbon Fight for Life holds special significance for an unlikely reason. 'That glove cost me about $12,000,' he laughs. 'I was the auctioneer that evening, and my dear wife made the winning bid. She got a bit too keen. I actually had to stop the auction because it got to the point where she started bidding against herself.'

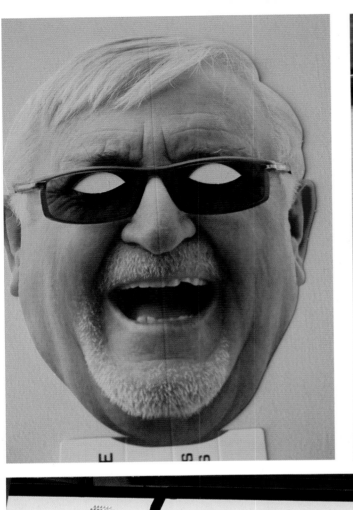

Man lamb burger

SERVES 6

For the burger patties
1kg lamb mince
1 onion, chopped, cooked in a little olive oil in a
   pan until soft and a little caramelised
2 cloves of garlic, chopped or grated
150g freshly grated breadcrumbs, soaked in just
   enough milk to moisten it
a small handful of fresh rosemary and mint,
   chopped (or 1 tsp of each, dried)
a splash of Worcestershire sauce
a few drops of Tabasco sauce
1 tsp smoked paprika
2 tsp sea salt
a few twists of freshly ground black pepper

For assembly
6 burger buns
your favourite mayonnaise
Iceberg lettuce leaves, washed and dried
2 Beef tomatoes, sliced
cornichons, sliced (optional)
sliced tinned beetroot (optional)
your favourite tomato chutney

Mix all of the burger pattie ingredients together,
divide into 6 balls, then flatten them into
patties slightly larger than the buns (to allow for
shrinkage).

Toast the buns on a barbeque grill (or
toaster), while cooking the patties on the griddle
(or in a frying pan) until well coloured on the
outside, and just a little pink on the inside.

To assemble, spread some mayo on both
bun halves, then on the bottom halves stack

on the lettuce, tomato, cornichons, beetroot,
a pattie, a dollop of chutney and the bun tops.

Variations
Add a fried egg to the stack.
Add a slice of cheese to the top of the patties for
the last minute of cooking.
Swap the lamb for beef, pork, venison or
chicken mince.

John

SLEEP RADIO

A heart attack and five resulting coronary bypasses left John with depression. 'A side-effect of which is this wonderful thing called "insomnia",' he explains. 'It was at its peak around three years ago while I was working as an HR manager for the Defence Forces. I would just stare at my computer all day. I didn't know what was going on. The sleepless nights turned me into a zombie.'

A counsellor recommended that John listen to some relaxation music. 'I didn't even like Elton John,' laughs the retiree. 'I downloaded some tracks: the Good Sleep music genre is Ambient. No lyrics, no loud music, no advertising, no announcers.'

With 18 years' experience as a projectionist in a Queen Street cinema, John was well-versed in electronics and sound engineering. 'I decided to sit down and find out what was involved in setting up a radio station. That was the hardest part. It took about three months to figure it out.'

The next hurdle John encountered were the legalities of sourcing music. 'I initially bought a few CDs, until finding out about copyright laws. I no longer have to go hunting for the music, because Ambient is one of the hardest genres to get airplay, so artists actually send me links to download their tracks. I reject around 50 per cent of it, because it might contain a beat or vocals, basically anything that might distract the listener from putting their head on the pillow and nodding off to sleep.'

It has to be slow and downbeat.

'I built a website, bought the domain name "Sleep Radio" and put my station on-air. Within days, the listening numbers went up and up. With internet radio you can see who is listening around the world.'

Most of the listeners are from the United States, Europe and, of course, New Zealand. John has ingeniously found a way of helping hundreds of people, without having to leave his front doorstep. 'I've been amazed at how successful it's been. I've been interviewed by health journals and various podcasts around the world. We get some fabulous feedback from listeners telling how much we've helped them. It's tremendously satisfying.

'There's nothing worse than struggling to sleep. Being grumpy, feeling irritable, and then dropping off in the middle of the day. Funnily enough, I've never had any difficulty getting off to sleep. My problem was that two hours later I would wake up. And apparently when I'm asleep I snore like a train.'

Sleep Radio, which costs John about $1000 annually to run, has a free app now, which can be downloaded onto smartphones or tablets. 'It's even got a sleep-timer, too. So you won't wake up in the morning with a flat battery. And it doesn't cost a bean.'

John also moonlights as a disc jockey once a week for an American radio station, broadcasting live from his home studio. 'I do a three-hour stint on a station in Kansas City called KCIA. They're a low-powered FM radio station in Kansas, Missouri.

'I answered an advert, and they let me choose my hours. They're 18 hours behind us, so I do their Tuesday evening: midday to three, our time. It's actually quite convenient. Their promo for me is hilarious: "Tune in to Kiwi John on Tuesday nights — and if you can get by that stupid accent, then you'll love him!" '

Raglan Bill

THE COVE

The Cove is an addition to the side of Raglan Bill's home. The basement, which was once the residence's concrete water-tank, adjoins a rustic, well-equipped workshop. 'Rainwater from the roof used to fill this whole room, and the water was pumped upstairs into the house,' he explains. A large fridge sits in the former reservoir. 'I stuck a map of Raglan on it so I don't get lost!' he roars.

'My old lady used to park her car in here. I actually built her coffin. She said she wasn't paying those bloodsuckers a cent. Undertakers, lawyers and land agents: they're all bottom-feeders in my book. I made my father's coffin out of tanalised ply — it was the only material I had at the time.

'The old lady's coffin was a pine box. I fitted the handle all the way around so everyone could carry it, even her grandkids. All the brothers and nieces would come down here and climb in to have a go. We would put the lid on and then whip a drill out and whack some screws in,' he cackles.

'My mum used to park her car in here, too. I concreted another few metres and added the fireplace. It wasn't quite big enough, so a mate of mine came down and welded a hoe head on the side that you can sit a poker in. Then welded a bit more on the other side. Now we cook on it. In winter it gets so hot when it cranks up that you have to sit here with the door open. It still leaks in here when it rains, and the fire steams.

'But that's good for the tobacco, because it likes a bit of moisture,' says Raglan Bill, pointing towards the ceiling and his drying tobacco leaves. 'I've been doing it for a couple of years now, and smoke all my own stuff.

'After the old lady died, we had a boat in here, and later I fitted a door. My mate Doug suggested we line the walls with punga. He brought the punga from his farm. Doug reckoned the lower wall would look good clad in rocks. I hadn't done rocks before, but he brought a load from the farm. I got some cement and we got cracking.

'We put the window in and hung the door as well. For a guy who doesn't smoke dope, Doug has the craziest bloody ideas. We fitted a triangle window in the upper part of the door and mirror-lined it, so we can peer out but outsiders can't see in.

'I like to create stuff out of recycled timber. At the moment I'm building starling boxes out of packing cases from the wind farm. I'm always working on projects in here. You can only do so much gardening. I will do a run on starling boxes, and then revert back to making knives or swords.'

Raglan Bill's impressive array of handiwork includes bread boards, rolling pins and rustic-looking mirrors, while custom-work has included a surfboard-shaped coffee table and a trophy for the annual Raglan Smoked Fish competition.

'Usually there's plenty of dust in here, although you're quite lucky I gave the place a sweep-out this morning.' He smiles. 'I've just been making axe-handles out of puriri. Cut them out with the jigsaw, then stick 'em in the fridge for eight weeks to dry out. The wood came from a bloke who chopped down a puriri tree in his backyard.'

Raglan Bill happily shows me two teeth he's had extracted from his mouth recently, before producing a tray full of spikes off the back of a shark from the local harbour. 'I'm going to turn them into earrings. Made so many last year I got sick of them.

'Everyone who visits here gets a present. That's my rule.' I am duly presented with a handmade spoon and a lethal-looking fly-swat, complete with bamboo handle and the words *DIE FLY* emblazoned across the black leather pad. The bugbear of selling his wares at markets are customers who constantly want to haggle. 'I can't be bothered,' Raglan Bill states bluntly. 'If you don't want to pay the asking price, then just piss off.

'A lot of my mates work in town, and they don't get back until after five. So I have a few handles down at the club, and then get back here around six-ish. My missus made me have a big feed at lunchtime and a small feed at tea. Changed my habits a bit. But I still like to knock the top off a couple.'

Raglan Bill proceeds to show me some of his prize Mantiques, including an 1856 Colt Navy pistol. 'That and the double-barrel shotgun behind it, which is an old flintlock, and the Winchester hanging over there, all came off the brother's farm in Colville. They were covered in concrete, but I cleaned them up and got them working. They're the reason the Maoris lost. The Maoris had muskets, but the Pakeha had six-shots.' Nearby sit a vintage pair of explosive wedges, found in a Ngahinapouri paddock, used for log-splitting.

Raglan Bill's personality does have its critics. A foray into local radio ended rather prematurely. Beeping out a constant torrent of colourful language proved too difficult a task even for the most experienced DJ. 'There were a few complaints,' he winces mournfully. 'If you don't like what you're hearing, then just turn the bloody radio off.'

On another occasion Raglan Bill, impersonating Corporal Klinger of the 4077th MASH, was dressed from head to toe in drag while riding on the local chemist's float in the town's Christmas Parade. For reasons known only to himself, he chose to moon one section of the crowd. 'I was even wearing a crocheted Willie Warmer, but some old girl still complained. We got first place, though, so must have been doing something right,' he laughs.

Raglan Bill regards mobile phones as the Devil's work. 'I've had a few, but given them all away,' he concedes. 'Apart from the one I threw off the wharf one night. I've got a landline if you want to get hold of me. If I'm not at home, it goes to answerphone. Simple. And if I like you, I might even ring you back.'

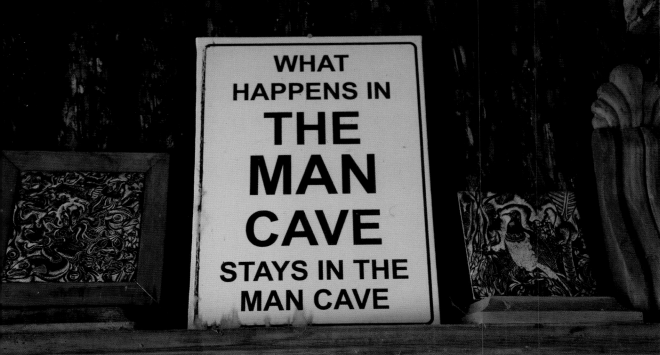

WHAT HAPPENS IN **THE MAN CAVE** STAYS IN THE MAN CAVE

RETURN TO SENDER

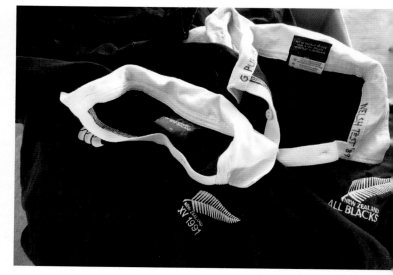

'No one ever really wants to swap their first test jersey, but after my All Black debut against the US Eagles at the 1991 World Cup, my opposite, Chris Lippert, pestered me,' recalls Graham Purvis, while teetering on the ladder en route to the attic. 'I'd actually packed away one of my reserves jerseys in anticipation of a swap.

'I must have had a weak moment and felt sorry for Lippert, who hobbled in on crutches to the All Black sheds. He told me he might never play again and really wanted the jersey I had worn that day. So I gave it to him thinking "So be it, that's life."'

Fifteen years later, Purvy received an email from a Kiwi who had been coaching in the States, relaying the information that Chris Lippert was trying to track him down. 'We communicated by email. Chris said he wanted to return my 1991 jersey, and felt guilty taking it off me. I said I would be delighted to have it back, of course, but on the condition that I could give him another All Black jersey of mine. To cut a long story short, we eventually met up, exchanged jerseys, and have kept in touch ever since.'

The attic excursion results in three large boxes being lifted down to the guest bedroom below. Several minutes of rummaging sees the prized jersey uncovered, along with many other treasures. 'Somewhere in here there should be a teddy bear that Mohamed Al Fayed gave me when the 1993 All Blacks visited Harrods.'

As the boxes' contents are emptied, various mementos, including touring ties, programmes, playing jerseys, even an invitation to Buckingham Palace (the Queen was lovely, by the way, and enjoyed a few Gs & T with the 1989 All Blacks) begin to engulf the Purvis upper spare bedroom, which soon resembles an episode of *Hoarders*. There are a few red herrings. Purvy's 1992 Waikato Rugby kitbag is bulging at the seams … with toys … Action Men, to be precise.

'I went through a bit of a stage when I was playing in France that I would regularly "souvenir" items that I liked. On the walls of the train stations there would be awesome stuff, like bull-fighting posters. I used to "collect" the best ones.

'I've got a few bits and pieces hanging up in here, mate,' says Purvy, entering his little den. 'The old front row are over there,' says the former Waikato and All Black prop, pointing to a framed photograph of himself, Warren Gatland and Richard Loe preparing to pack down against the 1986 touring Wallabies.

A large framed Fight for Life montage reminds Purvis of the night he made his debut in the ring, live on Sky TV against former Kiwi league player Brent Todd. 'That was a bit of fun. All the rugby guys, including Frank Bunce, Peter Fats (Fatialofa) and myself did a lot of training to prepare for that. I was travelling up to Auckland during the week, to a gym in Mount Eden, sparring against all sorts of crazy guys,' he smiles. Despite a deserved reputation for being one of the hard men in the provincial rugby of his era, off the field a grin is never too far from the Purvis dial.

Music, or more specifically singing along to string instruments, is another noted repertoire in the Purvis skillset. 'My father used to teach music — piano and guitar. I wasn't a very good student of my father's, although my brother was good enough to give me a few pointers. Anyway, we always had musical instruments lying around. I started playing the ukulele, and progressed on to guitar. On rugby trips the guitar at the back of the bus becomes a lot of fun. On tour you'd play the guitar a lot to kill a bit of time. More recently I've becomes reacquainted with the ukulele.

'I don't necessarily think I'm a very good singer, but I can remember a lot of lyrics. If you can play the tune and know the words, that's always a very good start, isn't it? And I've always maintained that, by that stage of the evening, you're singing for your own pleasure, not anyone else's.'

MIKE'S MUSIC ROOM

'Altogether I spent three and a half years working and travelling my way around Africa. I bought the one-piece wooden carving over there in "Rob-You-Blind-E", also known as "Nairobi",' says Mike, who is standing in a small, red-brick-clad sun-trap, where the Blues guitarist loves to practise. 'This room's got a nice little sound for echo. I put some new strings on my guitar last night and headed in here for a bit of a play. The acoustics are great.'

One special guitar in Mike's collection was handmade and gifted by a good friend. 'A friend lent one of his handmade guitars to me. I ended up looking after it for quite a long time. When he finally got around to picking it up, which was a couple of years after my fiftieth, as a surprise he said he would swap it for this one. So he handed me a case containing a custom-made guitar. It's a beautiful thing.

'It was created at a guitar-making school in Australia, from myrtle, which is probably also the name I'm going to call it as well.' He grins. 'It's been made with the best materials, even the Fishman pick-up is top of the range.'

Mike has had the barber-shop chair for about 25 years, purchasing it off a guy in Hamilton who needed to sell a few of his toys so he could get a mortgage. 'It's a Koken, so early American from around 1905, I understand.' German-born United States immigrant Ernest Koken first designed the hydraulic chair, to the eternal gratitude and admiration of barbers worldwide.

A Jimi Hendrix etching on display leads on to another interesting yarn. 'I had a spell working in the States for a mate while I trained to be a civil engineer. I was at a party over there after attending a BB King concert. I met this woman and we began talking about music. I told her about a Stevie Ray Vaughan photo I took at his concert at Hammersmith in 1988. She told me she'd swap me for a copy of an etching she had taken of Jimi Hendrix's headstone. So we swapped addresses, I sent her the photo and she came through, which was great.' Mike points out something quite special in his photo of Stevie Ray Vaughan. The iconic musician was actually wearing a Maori matau, or fish-hook carving, around his neck. 'His girlfriend at the time,' Mike explains, 'was a Kiwi.'

From tin Coca-Cola billboards to vintage racing bicycles, carved African figurines and retro hand-painted shop-front signage, Mike's home has become a piece of art. I would like to point out, everything seems in perfect order, individual artefacts are strategically placed — there is no evidence of clutter — and there's a noticeable absence of dust.

Fuelled by his travels, Mike has become something of an obsessive-compulsive collector. He seems to have his addiction well under control at this point in time, though. Slightly worryingly, however, Mike mentions that he may have to start using one of the empty sheds on his property just to 'start storing stuff' ...

Marty

THE CROCK
AND BULL

'When I got up to play the harp at my work do in 2015, that was the first time I'd played in front of anybody. I definitely shocked a lot of people,' ponders Marty while tuning his harmonica in The Crock and Bull. 'There were about 480 people present. The CEO challenged me. He said he didn't play the guitar in front of people, but he would if I played with him … Well, I've never been one to back away from a challenge. We played John Denver's "Country Roads".'

While his reputation as a pig hunter precedes him, Marty's musical acumen has been honed through many nights in the bush. 'My dad actually got me a harmonica when I was about seven. I played with it off and on over the years. I actually come from a really musical family. I had a seven-foot cousin who was a very good saxophone player, and my mum was right into piano.

'When I was culling pigs, I worked with a guy who played guitar. We could drive to our camp, so he took his guitar with him and we would jam together at night. One time we climbed into a helicopter to another location where we would be staying for three months. The pilot said there was no room for his guitar, which I thought was a bit harsh. So I was the only one with an instrument on that trip. That cemented my love for the harmonica. Every day for three months I could pull out my instruments and drive him nuts.

'I have played alone in the bush while the dogs rested during pig hunts. Great thing about the harp, you can take it anywhere.

'Back then, when you heard a harmonica it was always the Blues being played. I chose not to, because that's what everyone tends to play. I made a point of learning songs from start to finish and playing single notes. There's so much you can do with a harmonica — you can bend notes and make it talk.

'It's like a floodgate opening: the songs I've never played before, I can hear them and play that. Find the right key and away I go.

'One piece of helpful advice I was given is to purchase the best-quality instrument you can afford. Spend your money wisely. The trouble with a lot of musos, especially young ones, is they go and buy a cheap guitar or harmonica. So they start practising, and after a while they realise they sound terrible. They get disinterested, chuck the instrument in the corner and never play again. When you go from a sub-par instrument to a good one, your quality of sound changes immediately.

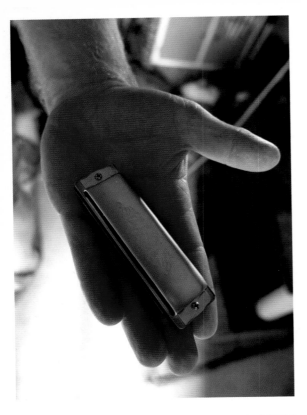

'I'm 100 per cent self-taught,' Marty reveals. 'I didn't know any other harmonica players I could go to for advice. I don't even hold the thing properly.' He laughs. 'I don't tongue-block properly … A lot of people in life get hung-up on how things are done, even if the end result is right. Find a way that works for you and go with it.'

The rustic Crock and Bull, headquarters of the Waitoki Pig Hunting Club, now doubles as a live music venue. If you look closely enough, guitars, a ukulele, drums, amplifiers, even a set of maracas can be found amongst the rows of jawbones, mounted heads and gin-traps. 'We have mates who come round here with guitars or drums for a jam. I play every day now. It's weird. If I don't play my harmonica daily, I walk around with a feeling almost like I haven't brushed my teeth.

'I don't look at it as practice; I just love playing it so much. I find something difficult to play and keep plugging away until I've got it down pat.'

Playing live, which he now does regularly, doesn't hold any trepidation. Performance anxiety doesn't seem to be an issue. 'I actually feel really good because I'm not up front. Lead guitarists and drummers deflect all the pressure off me.'

Marty admits he spends more time on the harmonica than pig hunting these days. 'Definitely. But I still take the harp when I do go hunting. I might have one in my pouch, and I will sit down in the bush while waiting for the dogs and pull the old harmonica out.'

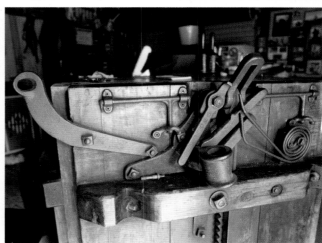

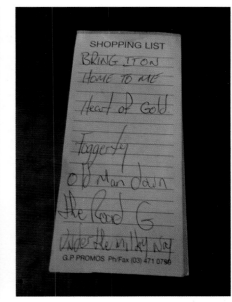

'EVERY NIGHT AFTER DOING
A DAY'S WORK, WE COME
BACK HERE TO LIGHT THE FIRE,
AND GET SOME MEAT AND
VEGES SORTED OUT. THEN,
WHILE DINNER'S COOKING,
ENJOY A NICE COLD BREW. '

Sausage 'n' hot slaw

SERVES 6

12 of your favourite gourmet sausages
   (ie, real meat, no fillers)

Slaw
1 tbsp olive oil
1 small onion, peeled, halved, finely sliced
2 rashers of streaky bacon or pancetta or
   chorizo, sliced

300g cabbage, finely shredded
50g carrots, chopped to matchsticks or grated
sea salt and freshly ground white (or black)
   pepper
1 tsp Dijon mustard
1 tsp grainy mustard
1 large tbsp mayonnaise

Fry off the sausages, then turn off the pan or put them to the side of the barbeque grill, while you get on with cooking the slaw.

Heat the oil in a pan or on the barbeque flat plate, and fry off the onion and bacon, until the onion is soft and caramelising around the edges. Add the cabbage and carrots, season and cook quickly, tossing about until just starting to wilt.

Add the mustards and mayo, tossing all together until evenly combined.

Serve immediately topped with sliced sausages.

Chef's tip
Do serve the slaw immediately, as otherwise the heat from the pan/plate will continue to cook it, transforming it into a soggy mess everyone loves to hate.

Mike

MISTER MIKE

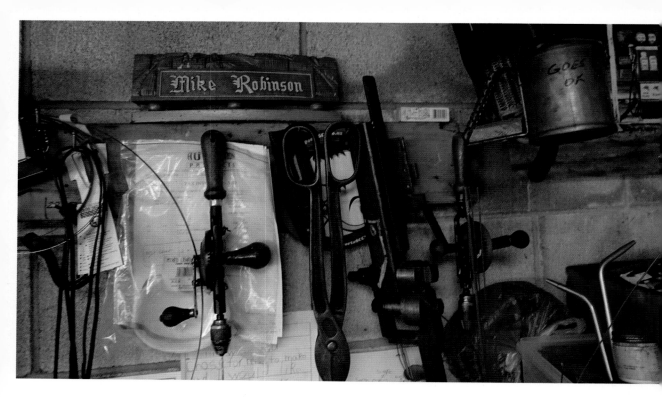

Mister Mike is the living epitome of the term 'paying it forward'. From his garage workshop he happily spends his spare time teaching boys the intricacies of engineering while also imparting the odd social skill. 'The boys come round here to my workshop after school. I try to teach them a bit of courtesy as well,' he smiles.

'I've loved teaching boys how to weld,' reflects the man who has forged an impeccable professional reputation for his precision engineering. 'They keep turning out all sorts of weapons. Swords, bows and arrows, high-powered potato guns, even an Aboriginal throwing spear called a woomera. Go-carts and motorbikes are also popular projects.'

'Mister Mike' has diligently recorded examples of his young protégés' extraordinary progress in albums, which he keeps on a shelf in the workshop. He has photos of 9- to 10-year-old protégés plasma-cutting 6-millimetre steel plate, and another snapshot of an eight-year-old turning a job on a centre lathe with a steely focus that belies his age. A height chart plotting the growth of his 'apprentices' over the years is etched onto the workshop door.

'I'll happily run these kids anywhere in the weekend, to their rugby or cricket or fishing or whatever, to keep them off the roads.' Turkey shooting and kayaking are

other weekend pursuits Mister Mike has overseen for his young crew. 'There have been a few hiccups along the way with a few. I've met with teachers, principals and police on occasions, and also managed to gain a reasonable understanding of how our court system operates in New Zealand. But they know, even if they do things that make me very sad, that I will never turn my back on them. They can count on that.'

Mister Mike arrived in New Zealand via flying-boat in 1946 as Michael Frank Long Robinson. Frank Long was a New Zealand bomber pilot; Mike's mother married him three months before he was killed over Holland. A subsequent marriage, which broke up in the war years, produced Mike. It would be many years before he would discover his unknown father and be reacquainted with an older brother.

'After leaving school I completed an apprenticeship in Seaview, Lower Hutt, as a fitter and turner. Then I joined the Merchant Navy — Port Line — as a junior engineer after finding out I had a father in England.' Docking in Liverpool, Mike took a train to London and was delivered to a residence in Earl's Court by taxi, where for the first time he met his father, who at that time was a producer with the BBC.

After leaving the Merchant Navy, marrying Elspeth and retraining, Mike spent nine insightful years as a psychiatric nurse, before returning to engineering. Being made redundant at the age of 56 didn't deter Mike in the least — he launched his own highly successful business, specialising in ultra-high-pressure water-blasting, which includes producing the mini blasting lances that wash the latticework high up on the Sky Tower … all from the sanctuary of his Man Cave!

Mike's engineering prowess is constantly in demand, whether it be motorbike frames that require welding, repairs on rifles, or custom projects. 'At 73 I've slowed down now. Two years ago I asked two of my commercial customers for less work so that I can spend more time with the boys. These days I usually knock off at 2.30pm so I can get down to the school in time to pick up the troops.

'I also encourage the boys with their rugby, cricket and other sports. It's good for the parents to realise how much it means if they can find the time on Saturday mornings to watch their sons play sport. I grew up without a father or elder brother, and I felt lost during my teenage years.'

Mike reveals that while training to become a psych nurse he began to understand his own feelings as an adolescent. 'I wondered why I hadn't been told some of these things as I was growing up. I feel really fortunate that I'm able to work with these boys and help them on their path. My sons have long since flown the coop, but my two grandsons are a great enjoyment. If I'm being selfish, I guess I feel grateful to have these boys and all their energy around me.

'Only months before going to see and discover my biological father, the greatest event of my life occurred. I encountered the Lord Jesus Christ and began a whole new way of life. The workshop and youngsters who frequent it continue the blessings I'm so grateful for.'

Our society lauds celebrities: we put the rich and famous on pedestals while marvelling at the feats of élite athletes. In reality, it's unassuming selfless individuals, like Mike Robinson, who make our world a better place. We need more Mister Mikes.

Phillip hand at it 2013 (early in year)

...shed ...cult ...n 2013

Blake and his wet weather conversion (Before it checked in on) 15/3/14

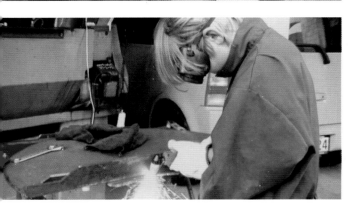

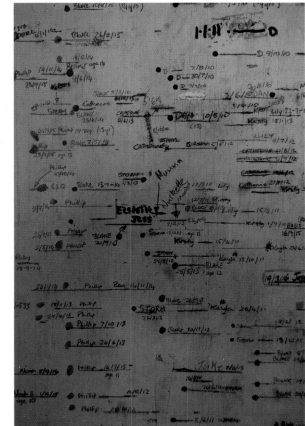

Blood

THE
BLOODSHED

One could be forgiven for thinking at first glance that the Bloodshed has been uprooted from some Louisianan backwater bayou. An old boiler, complete with chimney, smoulders away out front, while a smorgasbord of artefacts — including old brewery signage, sets of skis, a hanging birdcage, pharmacist's scales, lifesaver rings and sets of cricket stumps — clutters the rustic front porch.

Huge canvas advertising hoardings of Colin Meads, The Southern Men and a tin National Bank logo provide the backdrop, as do swordfish fins, a dolphin's skull, an early-model jet-ski, and a telephone pole to which dozens of early-model mobile phones have been nailed.

'Everything in here has been either collected, given to me or stolen,' confesses Blood. 'There's a story about every item, most of them believable and a few I can't tell you.'

Blood started collecting rugby memorabilia, but his Man Cave now includes kudu (an African antelope) and rhino horns, a ferret, surfboards, skis, cane fishing rods, boxing gloves, antique golf clubs, beer taps, even helicopter parts. An altimeter ripped out of an Iroquois sits on the coffee table. Blood has enlisted a fearsome, mobile security system to oversee his collection: a four-square Rottweiler called Raz, named after Shiraz, his owner's favourite drop.

Pinetree Meads opened the Bloodshed on 21 December 2002, the date and occasion confirmed by a plaque on the front porch. 'Funny story about that.

I was actually on the terraces for the opening of Waikato Stadium earlier that year. I managed to blag my way into the function room of the main stand. Went from cheap red wine to Stella. Anyway, I saw Colin Meads and waited for a lull to have a chat. I picked my moment. Pinetree said he would be delighted to open my shed. On the big day, Colin and his wife, Verna, actually stayed here for nine hours and looked reluctant to leave. I've kept the quart bottles he drank. They will never be swapped. His brother, Stan, has been a guest here, too.' Sir Colin Meads along with Sir Edmund Hillary and Sir Peter Blake are three of Blood's heroes. He has plans to commission an artist to paint portraits of the legendary Kiwi trio.

Inside an impressive display case in the corner stands a superbly taxidermied ferret (or 'roadkill', as Blood calls it). Above the vermin, in a frame hangs one of Aled de Malmanche's six All Black test jerseys. Blood struck up a friendship with the All Black hooker's father while their respective offspring rowed at school regattas.

Next to the jersey and above the large flat-screen TV hang sets of kudu horns, which Blood rescued from the rubbish pile of a neighbouring farmer. 'A lot of the stuff here has been salvaged from the transfer station. I guess after old blokes pass away plenty of their wives don't know what to do with their possessions, and just pack everything up into boxes and biff them.'

The red-and-black hooped rugby jersey, complete with leather reinforcing, which

BLOODSHED

RECEPTION

COURTROOM

hangs nearby, belonged to Blood's grandfather. 'I'm too scared to touch it,' he admits. 'It's so old and fragile.' Other iconic rugby memorabilia include Springbok and Cavaliers jerseys. All Blacks Brodie Retallick and Sam Cane visited recently, with the latter giving Blood one of his match-worn Chiefs jerseys. A Black Caps ODI sweater worn by Bryan Young and one of Ross Taylor's Central Stags helmets rest nearby.

Rhino horns hang above an old set of boxing gloves personally signed by the Tuaman. ('I was told he would be at the vineyard the night after fighting at Mystery Creek. I popped out there and got [David] Tua's autograph.')

Blood has carried the vintage mustard-coloured suitcase bearing a large Bob Marley sticker on many overseas rugby jaunts he has organised over the years. Memorabilia of each tour lines the walls. 'I entered a team in the Hong Kong Tens one year. Just a whole lot of broken arses from Ohaupo,' he laughs. 'Entry criteria depended on us having a number of high-profile players: I told a few fibs. When we arrived at Hong Kong, the organisers wanted to know where John Kirwan, Terry Wright and Zinzan Brooke were. I told them they were all injured. Funny thing is, we still finished second in our pool,' he roars.

Blood obtained his bar from a restaurant that went bust in Hamilton's main street, while the surfboards (which have been repaired and since used), fishing rods and wooden lure display cabinet came from R&R Sports who were relocating. He lined the interior of his shed while milling, and designed the trusses from macrocarpa on his property.

Blood loves entertaining visitors, who often add to his museum. 'Buying items for the collection does nothing for me. When you find something or have something given to you, it's so much more satisfying.'

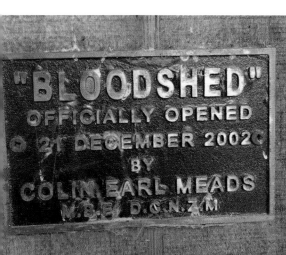

"BLOODSHED"
OFFICIALLY OPENED
21 DECEMBER 2002
BY
COLIN EARL MEADS
M.B.E D.C.N.Z.M

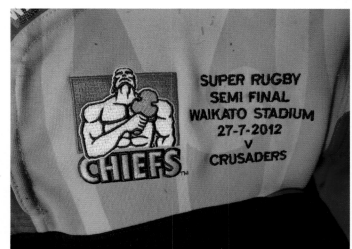

CHIEFS

SUPER RUGBY
SEMI FINAL
WAIKATO STADIUM
27-7-2012
V
CRUSADERS

WARNING

THUGS
POSING AS
CONTRACTORS

Please
RETURN EMPTIES
TO THE BAR...

"Stryd van die Reuse"
"Battle of the Giants"
1986 N-SEELAND TOER
1986 N ZEALAND TOUR

of a bullshitter
myself, but
occasionally I

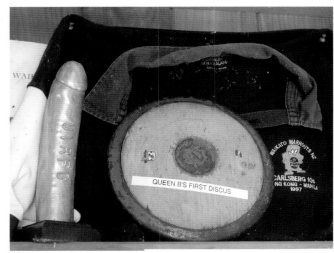

QUEEN B'S FIRST DISCUS

CARLSBERG 10s
HONG KONG - MANILA
1997

Glen

THE
CARPENTER'S
ARMS

'During my OE, I lived in Fulham, London. There was a shelf that ran all the way around our lounge: I thought it would be perfect for displaying beer cans. Of course in England there is a huge selection to choose from, so I would go down to the bottle store every day after work and buy a different can … or cans.' Before Glen knew it, the shelf, which ran the perimeter of the lounge, was full. 'At that point I decided I might as well start collecting other things.

'There was a place over there,' the Hamilton caretaker explains, 'called "The Bar with No Beer", where you could buy used taps and bar memorabilia. Secondhand and new. A lot of it had come from old pubs that had shut down or were being renovated. I picked up this big fella with the pump on it,' says Glen, pointing to the antique Adam's Bitter bowser.

'I lugged it across London on the tube to get it home. I think I paid £70 for it. It's a manual pump, not gas-operated, and would just hook straight into a barrel of cider or a bucket of Sangria.'

After four years in the UK, it was time to return to New Zealand. Glen packed 13 tea chests, 3 containing personal belongings and 10 of them full of bar memorabilia. He admits that his collecting had got out of hand. 'It was ridiculous,' he laughs. 'I wanted to keep it all and had to get it home.

'This is actually my third home Man Cave build; one of them had a large fish-tank mounted under the bar as a centrepiece. The first one was sold with our last house — I thought it would coax a male buyer. Of course I stripped the bar of all my collectables before we moved on.

'The macrocarpa slab was bought from Hookers Saw Mill as you see it. I think I paid $300 for it and another piece. Spent quite a bit of time sanding the face, and I applied a few coats of furniture oil. I kept all the jagged bits, grooves and features on the edges — who wants to look at a straight line?'

After collecting beer cans, Glen moved on to procuring antique wooden rulers, which he has hung cleverly on a pair of chains, almost like Venetian blinds, by

the bar. His Wellman Bros & Co ruler bears the three-digit '149', one of London's earliest phone numbers.

After rulers, Glen moved on to caps, then ties, then number plates … He admits to always being on the hunt for new items. 'Even down at the local refuse station — they have a shop there. You can pick up handles and glassware for between 50 cents and $2. It's probably time to knock it on the head really, I think this is complete.'

In the same breath, Glen still admits to having a secret hankering for expansion. 'I don't want to lose any more land, though, so I will have to build up,' he states. Several chunks of the Berlin Wall provide a real talking point. 'It was pulled down before I got to Berlin: people were trying to sell it, but there was plenty left to scoop up.' Oktoberfest steins and German glass drinking boots also feature. 'My wife and I had to skull out of those during our Top Deck tour of Europe.' A quirky selection of porcelain ashtrays, quintessential British pub regalia, a vintage till and an array of bottle-openers fill shelves behind the bar.

Personal possessions of Glen's grandfather are treasured, including a magnificent top hat, still stored in its original custom-built case. The cleverly crafted ship in the bottle, one of many his grandfather produced, is a legacy of his time at sea.

French doors lead onto the sun-drenched outdoor courtyard, the focal point being another of Glen's creations: the pizza oven. 'My favourite pizza would have to be pepperoni,' he says.

Behind the oven is another little alcove, which Glen has cleverly converted into a She Shed. 'When we first took over the property the space had been set up as two dog runs. We've had chickens in here, the barbeque and the spa pool. It's like *Changing Rooms*,' he laughs. The cosy nook has now been transformed into a fully equipped She Shed for his wife and her friends to enjoy, complete with fish-tank and a sliding partition window to improve the ever-essential Feng Shui and indoor–outdoor flow.

Glen has created the ultimate inner-city relaxation zone, even though certain external factors are out of his control. 'I had my fiftieth here a few years ago: there was a big band set up and a marquee outside. Noise control came around at quarter to 11! And of course we had spent weeks setting everything up. My wife is an expert negotiator, and she bought us an extra 90 minutes. There's no time limit these days regarding noise complaints. I'd sent fliers and invitations out to the whole neighbourhood, but it was definitely someone local who still complained.'

Steve

THE DOG BOX

Waiouru Motors owner Steve has a rugby collection so captivating that it once made Buck Shelford (a stickler for timekeeping) late. 'Buck visited here. Big Bad Buck. He found out about The Dog Box through an old Navy mate. Buck was passing through on his way to Palmy to run a coaching clinic. He was only supposed to stop for a quick coffee, but ended up staying for four hours!

'I was always in the shit, so I thought I had better make a real good Dog Box,' says Steve, who formerly served in the New Zealand Navy when they had a base at Waiouru, about as far inland as you can find yourself in the North Island.

'I used to play rugby for the Navy about 30 years ago,' he explains, 'and had the bar in my house so that the team would come around here for the after-match function. One day a mate of mine gave me one of Zinzan Brooke's New Zealand Sevens jerseys to put up on the wall. And then gradually all of the boys started bringing round more stuff over time.

'A guy walked in the door once, looked around and said, "I've got just the thing for you. I've been looking for someone to give it to for years." He returned with a ball signed by the 1956 Springboks.' A postcard signed by every member of the 1924 Invincibles is another of Steve's favourite possessions. 'It belonged to a shearer whose great-great-grandfather was in the team. He had originally planned on giving it to the rugby museum in Palmerston North, but after meeting my brother and hearing of my collection he decided I should have it instead.

'I've tried not to buy things; it's easy to buy if you have the money. But it's far more satisfying to collect. My dream has always been to open a rugby museum — and if I win Lotto, I will.'

The adidas All Black ball signed by the 1986 New Zealand Cavaliers, who controversially toured South Africa in 1986, was gifted by a former serviceman. 'Another mate of mine, a Navy boy, got that for me when the Cavaliers were in Devonport prior to their departure. My mate lived up in Kaitaia. I asked him to send the ball down, but he insisted I drive all the way up to see him and get it. So three of us jumped in a car. It took nine hours to get there, then three days and 32 pubs before we made it home. All for a signed rugby ball,' laughs Steve.

Another signed ball has an intriguing background. 'Brian Lochore held an unofficial All Black trial against Ohakune-Karioi before the 1987 Rugby World Cup. Not many people knew about it. This was the match ball from that day.'

Steve has an extensive display of match-worn international kit, including iconic All Black and Springbok items. Pairs of socks belonging to Grant Fox and Naas Botha, two of the game's super-boots, sit side by side, while on a rack hangs an intriguing collection of Springbok apparel, including a rare white jersey worn against Ireland, and a 1951 shirt still in excellent condition.

'Some of my oldest jerseys came from a local guy, Larry, who still works here in Waiouru. He gave me three of his black jerseys. He didn't get on the field for the Maoris, but was selected for those games and sat in the reserves. Obviously in those days one of the starting XV would have to die before they left the field. But he was in the 1949 New Zealand Juniors who played the Springboks at Eden Park, and a Maori All Black.

'I played against the Classic All Blacks for the Red Bands, and got one of their jerseys. They auctioned all of them off afterwards. I got one for my mate, and this one which was worn by Steve McDowall. I tried to punch him during the game,' laughs the former feisty halfback, 'but Steve wouldn't have a bar of it. It was at a ruck — I've always wanted to punch an All Black. McDowall said, "Don't try it, bro, I'll give you a hiding."'

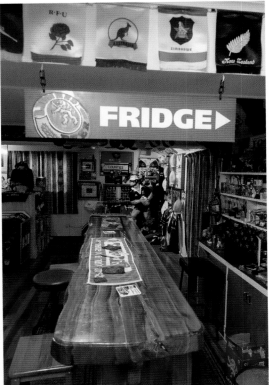

Aside from jerseys, Steve likes collecting unique pieces of rugby memorabilia. 'I really like all the knick-knacks you can find. Even my kids are contributing.' Steve points to a tiny carved wooden item. 'This is the only one made in the world. It came from Prague. My daughter saw a guy at a market who was making these American football and baseball and soccer player Russian-doll sets. She asked the guy if he could make a rugby version for her dad, so he carved this set overnight. Dan Carter number 10, then Kieran Read, Tony Woodcock, Keven Mealamu and little Piri Weepu in the middle.'

The zebra hide on the floor has an interesting story attached to it. 'It was actually presented by the South African President in 1949 to the touring All Blacks captain, Fred Allen. When Fred was redecorating his house many years later, he found it neatly folded in a box. He offered it to a friend of mine who was helping him, who asked if it would be alright to pass it on to me. Fred was fine with that. It's well-worn and a bit buggered, but should really be a museum piece.'

Another addition to The Dog Box came through a chance meeting with some out-of-towners at the local watering hole. 'These old guys were in the pub and we started yakking to them. They usually go up the Whanganui River on a yearly trip, but the road was closed so they stayed here. I brought them down to The Dog Box. One of the guys had played 47 games for North Auckland. Three days later he sent me his jersey.'

Three large, framed All Black team pictures were given to Steve by a customer at his garage in lieu of payment. 'A lady owed me money for the bill. The pub she was in in Rotorua had gone broke, so I did a deal and took the memorabilia instead.'

While Steve generally prefers not to pay for items, he made one notable exception, dipping into his pockets to support a worthy local cause for a ball signed by the 1982 New Zealand Maori side that toured Wales and Spain. 'The ball had been taken to kindergarten by a kid for show-and-tell,' he reveals. 'And obviously the kid forgot to take it home. It was put in a cupboard and found years later by the teachers, who asked me what they should do with it. I suggested they raffle it off as a fundraiser. They ran the raffle, I bought all 100 tickets on the spot at $2 each and took the ball straight home!'

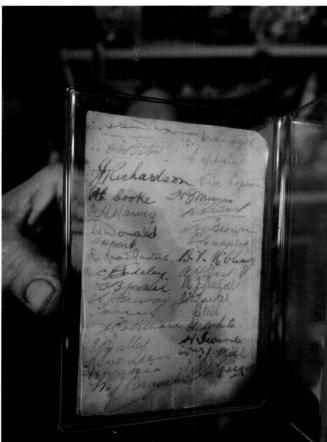

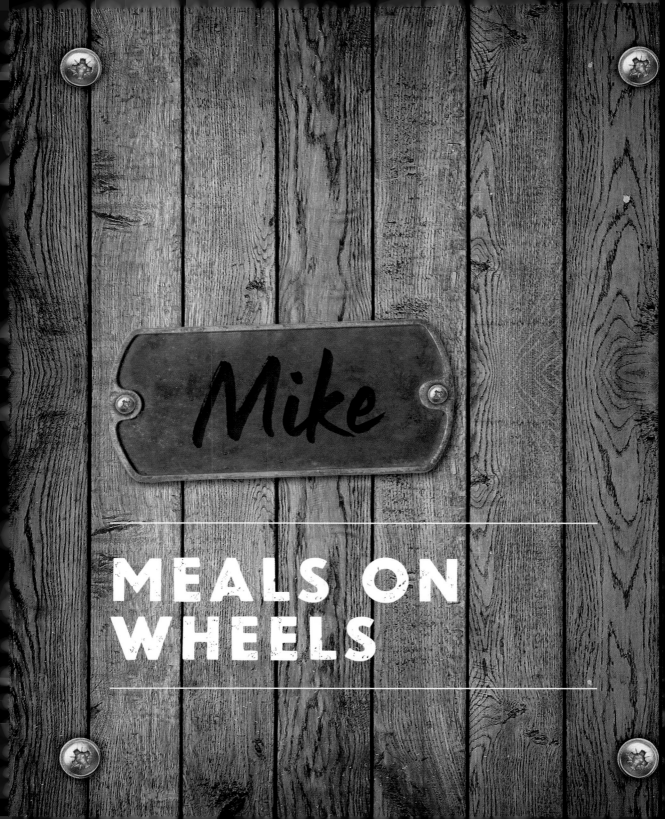

Mike

MEALS ON
WHEELS

When Tauranga man Mike returned to New Zealand after nine years of living and working in the UK, he somehow managed to convince his wife that they spend the money they had saved for their first house on a 3-tonne mobile Texas Smoker. 'I got Nadine on the white wines and talked her into buying a barbeque instead of a house,' he jokes. 'Once the decision was made, it was all go to set it up as a catering company. And we've been tormenting vegetarians ever since!

'You get a lot of funny looks towing a 3-tonne barbeque, especially when it's still smoking away. People tell me all the time that my trailer's on fire,' he laughs. 'I've towed it all over the country, even right up the top of the Coromandel. Been pulled up twice by the police, only because they want to know all about it. The funniest was after a function, and a few beers later, when I ended up having to get a dial-a-driver to get me and the barbeque home.'

It may sound a little excessive to the common man, but Mike regularly uses his barbeque for personal use. 'I usually wait until the neighbours put their washing out on the line,' he smiles, 'before stoking up the fire.

'Everyone's got gas barbeques at home. I can't stand it — just no flavour at all. Once you try a smoked barbeque, your taste buds will turn.' Mike makes up all of his own rubs and sauces, and even (wait for it) a bacon jam. 'One customer in particular just can't get enough of it. The stuff is like crack to him.'

Pohutukawa is Mike's smoking wood of preference. 'It's got a good, subtle flavour. Most people who smoke meat or fish use manuka or kanuka, but the smoke can be quite overpowering.' Sourcing limbs from the New Zealand Christmas tree requires stealth-like guile. 'You've just got to do it at night-time when no one is looking,' he jokes. 'Actually, there's a few arborists around town who supply it, and you can buy the odd load off Trade Me as well. The best wood I've used would have to be peach tree. It's got a great flavour. Anything like pine that has high amounts of resin is no good at all. Hardwoods are best.'

Mike's first foray into the catering world occurred when he was asked to sort the meat for a wedding. 'I was bloody nervous,' he freely admits. 'I couldn't sleep the night before. People loved it, though. American-style barbeque has become really popular here in New Zealand, and we're booked up over summer, mainly for weddings now.' The handlebar-mustachioed Mike can fit four whole pigs into his barbeque and cook a whopping 200 steaks an hour. 'If I'm doing a whole pig, that can be a 14-hour day. Patience is the key with slow cooking. It's quite a good job sitting back and cooking meat.'

Last year the big fella undertook a lengthy road trip of the United States, all in the name of 'professional development'. 'I've been to the Beer, Bourbon and BBQ festival in North Carolina, Oklahoma Joe's, 12 Bones, Jack Stacks in Kansas City … All the big ones.' Americans, it seems, take their barbequing very seriously indeed. 'When you go to Franklin's Barbecue in Austin, Texas, you've got to start queuing at 5.30am every day. No exceptions. Even a big-name celebrity like Kanye West was told to get to the back of the queue.' Mike appreciated the subtle differences between barbeque pedagogy as he explored the US of A. 'All of the states have their different flavours,' he explains. 'The Carolinas are vinegar-based, Kansas City-style is kind of sweet, while Texas is all about the beef.

'I've smoked all sorts of stuff, from duck to mussels, and eaten a lot of different shit, too. When I was in Romania there was bear on the menu. Had to try a bit of bear with my beer. I found it a bit chewy. I've had moose in Sweden, reindeer, and even ate a dirty, stinking pigeon in Egypt. I once stayed overnight in the desert in Jordan, and was surprised to find that their traditional style of cooking was a hangi. Not quite the same taste, though, on account of the sand.'

Admittedly, Mike is not the world's greatest advocate of the fresh fruit and vegetable 'five-plus a day' campaign. 'Maybe mushroom wrapped in bacon,' he suggests. 'I'm thinking about putting out a carnivore menu that includes five meats, possibly accompanied by a side coleslaw for a bit of green.

'It's been a lot of hard work over the past six years, but I can honestly say I love my job. I'm on my way to creating my "barbeque empire". Next up would be my own cookbook and TV show!'

Reuben sandwich

SERVES 3

For the Russian dressing
½ cup of your favourite mayonnaise
2 tbsp tomato ketchup
1 tsp Worcestershire sauce
1 tsp minced horseradish
a few twists of freshly ground black pepper
a pinch cayenne pepper
sea salt to taste, if needed

For assembling the sandwiches
6 slices rye bread (rye is best, but any will do, preferably buy an artisan loaf and slice it yourself)
500g pastrami or corned beef, thinly sliced
500g Swiss cheese (Emmental, Gruyère or Dutch Maasdam), thinly sliced
300g sauerkraut (pretty much most of 375g jar)
½ cup Russian dressing
a bit of butter for toasting

To make the Russian dressing, simply mix together all of the ingredients, and make any adjustments according to taste. Refrigerate any unused dressing. (It's just flavoured mayo, so it will last as long as your mayo does in the fridge.)

To assemble the sandwich, first lay out all of the slices of bread and spread them with a good dollop of the Russian dressing. On three of the slices, layer on the meat, cheese and smeared-on spoonfuls of sauerkraut in triple-decker fashion. Repeat, so that you have two layers of everything. Cover with the other three slices of bread.

Melt a little butter in a large skillet pan on the stove or on the barbeque griddle, and toast the sandwiches until nicely brown, pressing them down with an egg slice (or bacon press if you have one). Spread some butter on the top slices, then flip the sandwich over to brown this side, too, pressing down again. They are done when the cheese has reached your preferred degree of meltedness. Or if you have a sandwich/panini press, brush a bit of butter on both plates and bung them in this.

Mark

THE OFFICE

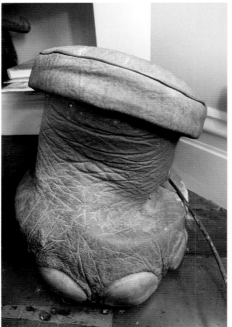

'It's eclectic in here, I suppose you could say,' ponders Mark, an icon of New Zealand journalism. 'I've got the dentist's light over there. The chair to go with it is currently up in my Auckland flat. I love all of that 1940s–1950s-era hospital, industrial-type stuff.'

Mark lets slip that he and his wife are avid op-shoppers. 'We ended up one Saturday going out to the Porirua Recycling Centre. "Trash Palace" they call it. And I saw the old Lancaster bomber hanging off the roof. It certainly wasn't a bargain. Some old boy had built this thing, and I bought it with my redundancy cheque from *Close Up*.' He laughs. 'You never worry about that sort of stuff.'

Ferrying the enormous model aircraft home proved to be quite an adventure. 'I ended up getting it into the back of a Hyundai i30 wagon after taking the wings off. My mate and I couldn't believe it fitted.' Hanging the plane required serious manpower. 'My mate Tom Scott came around. He's a big guy, and we had a couple of Swedish hitchhikers I'd picked up. It took about four of us to hang it off the ceiling. I just like it. It's really a bit nuts.

'The plane's body is made of polystyrene, and there are lots of working parts like the flaps. It may have been built as a flying model. There's a few bits missing, though, like the old nasals and propellers. I had another mate around one night who is a model-maker and makes things for Weta Workshop. He offered to restore it to its former glory. At some stage I will. One day … Like the guitar sitting in the corner, which I decided I would teach myself to play when I have a bit of spare time on my hands. It's come out of the case about four times, and that's when a cousin has come around to tune it up for me,' he roars.

'I guess I do really like odd, weird sort of stuff. There's plenty of that around Wellington.

'I went to South Africa because a mate was getting married, and as we were leaving we found a shop selling hides and skins. We checked with them about taking them out of the country. We got a certificate to prove the animal wasn't endangered. When we got to the airport I thought "Here we go", but it was checked thoroughly to ensure there was nothing hanging off, and it was given the all-clear.

'The elephant's footstool, which I know isn't terribly PC, came from my brother Peter, who picked it up at an auction. I know it's not the sort of thing you're supposed to have, but it was already dead — we didn't lop off a foot and have it made.

'I used to do quite a bit of writing in here. I remember a mate said to me that you've got to have your own space to sit so you can focus on what you're doing. And if you don't have that, you won't do anything. He's quite right.'

Mark originally bought the desk secondhand for his wife when she began her law practice. 'It has the old leather top and little storage doors, it may well have come from an old government department. I cleaned it all up, re-varnished and everything. She outgrew it, so I re-gifted it back to myself.'

A small scrapbook sitting on a shelf is a gem that Mark values dearly. 'I did a quiz night about five or six years ago for a school out at Laingholm and the kids all drew pictures of me as part of a project. It's really quite funny how kids see you. One drew me dressed up as a girl. Another one created me as Mr Potato Head. There's no pretence with kids, that's exactly how they see it. It's one of the most precious things.

'I love rockets and boats … and models as well,' he continues, pointing to a whaling ship to his right. Another item of 'slightly questionable taste', as he puts it, is an item purchased from the Smithsonian in Washington, DC. 'It's a photo of the *Enola Gay*, the plane that dropped the atom bomb on Hiroshima, signed by the pilot who flew her on that fateful mission. They had it in the gift shop. I thought what a weird thing it was to sell, which is exactly why I bought it.'

Mark is also an avid comic book fan: 'I've got the entire Zack collection — every one ever produced. And hundreds of Phantom comics.'

An original handmade poster from the Chinese Cultural Revolution is another talking point. 'I've done a bit of travelling and been to China a few times over the years, when I was political editor and during the *Close Up* days. I love that style of art,

and went to a poster museum. I found this one which was handpainted in 1967. It's such a nice piece. Or it's a fabulous fake.' He laughs. 'It doesn't really matter.

'If I'm here by myself, I will crank up the volume. I mainly listen to old stuff like The Doors, The Stones. I love old Blues and '50s stuff. It's hard to get past the stuff you grew up with. Doobie Brothers, Eagles … The kids used to complain, but suddenly you find they're listening to remakes of it with you.'

Everything you buy as an adult, Mark believes, traces back to the things you wanted when you were growing up but couldn't afford. 'I finally bought a Lincoln Continental, which I've always admired. I've kept a copy of *The Observer Book of Cars* since I was a kid. There are six boys in my family, and we all had favourite cars. The Lincoln was mine. I was determined that one day I would get one, and I finally did. I knew the car was arriving while I was at that wedding in South Africa, and, while I wouldn't have missed the wedding, I had been waiting my whole life for that car.' He grins. 'I was itching to get back home. The big thing that worried me was that I had been dreaming, thinking and searching for that car for so many years, that the wanting feeling was greater than actually owning it. I was so stoked when I finally saw it. I drive it every day I possibly can when I'm home in Wellington.

'You look at people who are filthy rich, and on one hand you think it would be great, but then you think if you can afford to have everything you've always wanted, there's no pleasure, no joy in it. When you get something you've set your heart on, there's a real sense of accomplishment, having to save up and pool all your money together.'

Steve

THE BULL'S
HORNS

Close the passageway door and I'm instantly divorced from the rumblings and chaos of the house. My office is a sun-trap blessed with a rural outlook (no, this is not a real estate advert).

Opening the French doors that lead to the deck lets birdsong engulf the room (while typing these words I can clearly hear the *pop, pop, pop* of duck shooters' shotguns), not to mention a cacophony of mooing coming from over the back fence. When the wind wafts this way I can smell the livestock, which, having lived in the country most of my life, is a reassuring, pleasant sensation.

The vast majority of the book you are currently reading (and hopefully enjoying) was penned at my recycled teacher's desk, which was salvaged from a skip. After sanding the surfaces back, several liberal coats of beeswax were applied. It exudes character (aka borer holes) and the odd indentation made by either an unruly student or an equally frustrated teacher. It's by no means a quiet worktop: the old legs creak loudly and frequently.

My pencil-holder is an authentic Canadian maple syrup tin brought to New Zealand by my Yukon friends, Shae and Camille. Apparently, my pancake recipe beats their flapjacks hands-down! The piece of schist positioned on the desk was a gift from my old mate Doomy, from one of his infamous Central Otago fishing trips.

The white double doors conceal my secret fetish: a collection of match-worn rugby jerseys. It took 20 years to get my dream shirt, an adidas French props jersey from the 1980s era. Then, before I knew it, I had two in a week. I'm extremely fortunate to have friends who have played code at a decent level, who have generously contributed to my stash. Collecting is a funny pastime. It's really hard to get started, but when your collection grows, all sorts of people start giving you amazing stuff. I've made some fantastic friends through collecting, like Big Bird Paterson, who is generous to a fault — and a few low-down crooks as well …

There's a lot of stuff plastered all over the walls in here; cool drawings by my kids, quotes, posters and photos. The two snapshots of the first two original paintings of mine that sold are special mementos for me. Unfortunately, both were later destroyed in a house fire.

A feature of my big pink bookcase is my complete collection of *DB Rugby Annuals* 1971–1993. I got a few for Christmas as a kid, and in my adult years I made it a mission to collect every edition, rummaging through car-boot sales, secondhand shops and white elephant stalls.

The top shelf also contains the Inspector Rebus series by Ian Rankin, including a book personally signed by the author, which I found in the bargain barrel of a Hamilton bookshop for just $15.

There's a few little keepsakes on display around the room that evoke pleasant memories, various rugby tankards I was awarded, two steins sneakily acquired from the Stump Bar in Lauterbrunnen, my Siam Cup player tie, a piece of bone a former workmate carved for me while serving time in the big house, tour tokens from the Guinness Storehouse, an old tattoo gun, and the smiley-face staff badge I wore on the door of the Hillcrest Tavern in the early 1990s.

The milking cup lights that Ben — a mate of mine, who is a sparkie — wired up have practically gone viral. People rave about them. There is a thick cable of black hose inside each section, so you can position and set the stainless cups individually, like spotlights. Our plan is to raid old cowsheds all over the Waikato and sell 'Kiwi Mantique' Dairy Cup Lights to the world. I reckon they will become iconic.

No mention of my office would be complete without referring to the Highland cow skull, which hangs above on two lengths of reinforcing steel. The head was supposed to be mounted, although my mate Jay, who did the slaughtering and

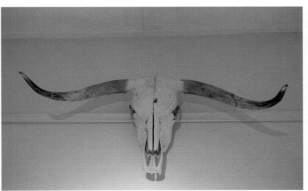

subsequent decapitation, didn't leave enough skirt (the neck, chest and upper back hide) for a taxidermist to work their magic. We ended up with a hairy, horny head complete with bulging eyeballs living in the bowels of our deep-freezer, which terrified my poor daughter whenever she ventured to the garage to get frozen goods for the evening meal.

To ease my daughter's nightmares, a local pig hunter kindly offered to store the decapitation in his wild pork freezer, where it stayed for another year. Subsequently, during that period of time I forgot all about it and just got on with my everyday life. Eventually, without my knowledge, the head was boiled down (burying for three months is another proven method) and given a polish. Needless to say, I was rapt with the end result. To complement the bovine theme that is fast developing in here, my next purchase is definitely going to be a bull-hide rug.

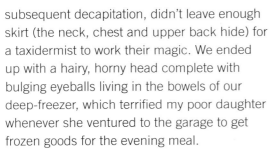

Pete

WHISKEY
FLATS

'I can come home on a Friday at 3pm after work and leave on a Monday morning at 8am. In that whole time I mightn't have even left my front gate,' says burly, bearded petrol-head Pete. 'I'm not on the tools anymore at work, but I can come out here and spanner away and get covered in grease like I used to for 30 years, and I'm more than happy. I go back to work feeling fresh.

'The original idea for the shed actually came from a photo I'd seen on the internet, of a place near Taupo with a couple of cars out front,' explains Pete, who by day runs a forklift-lease company in Rotorua. 'We've also visited heaps of old hot-rod sheds in the States. Cars and bikes have always been my thing,' remarks the former diesel mechanic, who now resides on the Eastern Bay of Plenty coastline.

'I only watch about an hour a week of television; the rest of the time I'm out here.' Regular reconnaissance missions by Pete and his wife to 'our second home',

the United States, refuel Pete's motivation to create and restore. 'We were even planning our next trip recently — before returning home from the last one.' Pete laughs.

Pete's shed was built, lined and decorated between trips to the States and restoring cars, bikes and trucks. 'About the only thing I didn't do was put the concrete down, but I gave the guys a hand. I stood all the trusses up. I didn't do the roof, but I did put all the purlins and guttering up.

'Typically, I have about 20 projects going all at once! I have to be in the mood, and when I am nothing else matters. Like when I did the pick-up truck, I'd be out here every night and weekend. I can do most of the work myself, like welding, but I get a few mates to do any major fabrications.'

Pete is currently erecting a full-size windmill on a concrete pad in his backyard. While old-school America is a recurring theme, there's also a healthy dollop of

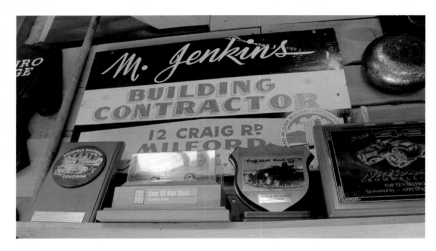

technical wizardry on-site. Like the ingeniously wired sensor that kick-starts Pete's exterior and interior neon signage, spectacularly illuminating his garage for two hours upon dusk.

'Whiskey Flat was originally an old gold-mining town back in the cowboy days. It's at the base of the Sierra–Nevada mountain range near Bakersfield in California. They shifted the town of Whiskey Flat further down the valley, and it's now called Kernville. When we go over, we always try to catch up with friends, attend hot-rodding events and swap-meets.'

Not even an intellectual mastermind the level of Stephen Hawking would be able to logically process and order the array of vehicles, artefacts and signage on display in Pete's impressive collection. 'I've brought back boxes and boxes of stuff from the States.'

A complete set of American licence plates screwed to interior walls and trusses were given to Pete by a former LAPD cop he met at an alley party, while the giant portrait of Johnny Cash giving the bird was picked up from a swap-meet in Paloma. The 'carousel', which Pete fashioned out of empty Corona boxes, was a throwback to the way grocers used to stack empty chewing-gum cartons.

'There's a small story to a lot of the stuff here. A couple of the items hanging on the walls really mean a lot to me. One is the sign for my deceased uncle's truck. He was a bit of a mentor to me back in the day. A builder by trade, but he could lend his hand to anything. He could build stock-cars, little speedway cars. He never raced anything himself, but would always build things for other people. I have his first building sign over there, too, from when he came out of his apprenticeship and started his business.'

The yellow fire-hydrant from Kernville is one of Pete's more audacious purchases. 'An example of the dumb shit that you do when you're away,' he laughs. 'We were five hours from Long Beach, and I buy a fire-hydrant that you can't even lift to bring back to New Zealand. We tried to get it into the back of the rental, but we couldn't even pick it up.' Fortunately, on that same trip Pete had picked up a couple of pallets of engine parts, so a friend ensured the hydrant got onto a pallet for shipping home. Problem sorted!

An eye-catching row of vintage motorcycles (one of which was purchased as a substitute wedding ring for his wife, Tania) holds pride of place. 'I've taken the Indian down to the Burt Munro Challenge twice now and raced it on the beach at Oreti. It was hair-raising. The first year the tide was right up, so they had to shift the track into the soft stuff. With these sort of tyres, you're all over the place.'

Pete's connection to Burt Munro doesn't end there. He's also worked on a crew at Bonneville for racing legend Ed Newett. 'We went over there a week before Bonneville in 2005, and worked on his car in a retirement village. We spannered the car and did some wiring, we changed the ratio on the power, changed diff ratios … did a lot of work on the car, and helped them get a world record.'

Pete ended up going to Bonneville three years in a row, working with some of the legends of Californian hot-rodding. 'To be part of that was just incredible. We didn't realise how famous the guys we had been knocking around with actually were. They all know about Burt Munro.'

Pete has been involved in hot-rodding since the age of 18. He likens the community to one big family, a great gang to join. 'When you go to a long-time hot-rodder's funeral — fark, it's a huge event.

'When I'm on my death-bed, I want to have great memories. I've got great satisfaction from what I've achieved. You don't want any sort of public recognition. When you jump into bed at night after finishing a project, and you know you've created something special yourself, you sleep like there's no tomorrow. To me, that's what this deal is all about. Constantly buying brand-new just to make yourself feel better is shallow.'

THE
GREENZONE

'It was probably initially a rugby collection,' Kerry suggests. 'Every year the breweries and rugby union would put new posters out. I'd collect programmes and display the more collectable cans on the rafters of the garage. In the late 1990s when I was thinking about doing something, I decided to draw the line and concentrate on collecting items with either Waikato or Willie the Waiter on it. The rugby stuff all had the breweries logo on it as well.

'A mate of mine, Pete, who's a joiner, helped put together the bar, which actually used to be a bookcase. It's kauri. There are drop-lights fitted underneath. Another friend, a welder, found a bit of pipe in a cowshed, took it away to measure it all up, then fabricated the foot-rail. He brought it around. It was a hot day, we were both lying on the floor trying to bolt it in, and the sweat was pouring off us.'

Kerry bought the gleaming green beer fridge in the corner way back in 1974. 'My son who is a spray-painter said we should really do it up and paint it bloody green. He stripped it right back, which was a big job because it had four or five different coats of shit on it. The spigot has died; I'm on the look for a new one.

Someone suggested I cut a hole in the back and wire a sound system in, but I'd rather not. I will run into a refrigeration engineer one day who will be able to do something with it that doesn't cost the earth.'

The double doors are undoubtedly the show-stopping feature of Kerry's cave. 'I didn't know anything about the doors. My wife surprised me with them. I came home one day, the new house was just about finished, and I found two leadlight doors with Willie the Waiter on them. In 1945, a bloke by the name of William T. Waiter commenced employment at the Hamilton Brewery. By all accounts he was a popular individual, and his distinguishable facial features were later immortalised in caricature form by Waikato Draught.'

An enormous Waikato flag, which Kerry's wife sewed some backing onto, serves as an impressive curtain for the sliding door leading out to the main entrance. 'That actually came from Waikato Stadium. They were giving them out at one of the games in the late 1990s.' A macrocarpa block with *Kerry's Cave* engraved on it is secured to the exterior wall of his house, above an illuminated square of Waikato

Draught signage. 'My son fixed it up and gave it to me a couple of years ago. "What I've just given to you," he said, "is your Christmas present, Father's Day present and birthday present." I'm 60 now, and there's not many material things you really want. So I told the kids that if they're going to buy me something, find something that will go in here.

'We built the house back in June 2007, and this purpose-built space was always in the architect's plans. As far as my wife was concerned, the only thing I was interested in having was the Man Cave.' Kerry admits that there has been talk of knocking the back wall out to erect a grandstand so seating capacity can be increased for major rugby games.

'We probably only go to the stadium once or twice a year now, maybe one Waikato game and one Chiefs game. But it's pretty hard to leave here,' says the former Frankton Rugby Club stalwart. 'Get to the middle of August, when it's cold and grotty outside and Waikato are playing a home game, but the temperature's always the same by the bar in front of the television.'

The framed blue-and-black hooped jersey on the wall harks back to the 2012 Frankton club reunion. It was worn in the senior game played that day. 'The irony was I was a loosehead prop for Frankton. I got the green light from the missus to bid on the number 1 jersey, my old playing number, at an auction in the clubrooms on the Saturday night. Once the bidding hit $300 in $10 lots, I started to get cold feet. I pulled out of the bidding at $460, it was getting ludicrous.

'I realised the guy bidding against me wanted the jersey pretty bloody bad. I later found it was for his son, who was in the Frankton U15s and who'd had some sort of serious accident and couldn't play rugby anymore. It turns out his son also played loosehead prop. So I'm glad he got it. I bid for this jersey later that night, and got it for $160. Cheapest of the whole night. The club ending up making $8700 for the whole set.'

Kerry won the signed and framed Chiefs jersey from a Placemakers Ambrose Golf Tournament at St Andrews in aid of prostate cancer. 'That was another auction. I kept waving my hand in the air, and ended up getting it for $550. As I was driving home I was thinking, "Shit, how am I going to explain this one?" I decided that honesty was the best policy: I would tell her how it was. So I fessed up, and the reaction I got from my wife was great. Marryanne said she had been unsure what to get me for our thirtieth wedding anniversary — I actually solved her problem.' He grins. 'But I was also told not to make a habit of these spur-of-the-moment purchases.'

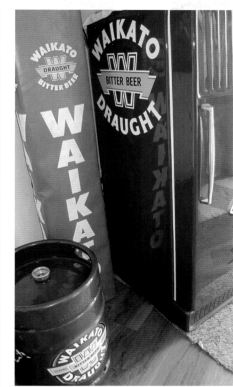

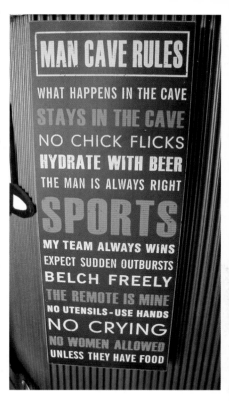

MAN CAVE RULES

WHAT HAPPENS IN THE CAVE
STAYS IN THE CAVE
NO CHICK FLICKS
HYDRATE WITH BEER
THE MAN IS ALWAYS RIGHT
SPORTS
MY TEAM ALWAYS WINS
EXPECT SUDDEN OUTBURSTS
BELCH FREELY
THE REMOTE IS MINE
NO UTENSILS - USE HANDS
NO CRYING
NO WOMEN ALLOWED
UNLESS THEY HAVE FOOD

Jono

THE
SKYSPHERE

After building a treehouse on his parents' farm in the Manawatu — no ordinary treehouse, mind you: this one had hot running water, a bath and a remote-controlled retractable gangplank — Jono still had a self-build itch requiring serious scratching.

Never one to shy away from a challenge, the 28-year-old design engineer, who by day specialises in the product development of plastic-injected moulding tools, decided to construct a 9-metre tower, which has become a welcome addition to the Aokautere skyline and can be seen by the naked eye from downtown Palmerston North.

'I started with a treehouse; that turned out quite well, so I decided to try something completely different.' The off-grid treehouse, built on the side of a steep bank from recycled materials, features in *Cabin Porn*, a book that has become essential reading for tiny-house builders worldwide. Jono's motivation is fuelled by two factors: 'I love engineering, and it's always good to have a project on the go in Palmy. There's not much else to do here!

'I always thought this would work,' insists Jono, who happily admits running into the odd hurdle. 'It wasn't quite as easy as I thought it would be, though. For example, some of the steel that arrived from China wasn't made to my specifications, the tolerances weren't correct. So I had to learn how to heat-form with oxyacetylene. I didn't even know how to weld initially, so I did a course at UCOL.' He admits that there were times when the project became frustrating and he took time off. Over the odd quiet drink he managed to nut out any problems and brainstorm viable solutions.

'I didn't really look or base this on anything else I'd seen. If you want to be original, you've got to go with what's in your head. I like to do my own thing. I like minimalism; as you can see, there's no light switches in here. Everything runs off my phone. I've invented colour mixes so that you can toggle between colour and brightness.' Jono put a bit of research into the dynamics of colour theory. For example, when you're feeling sleepy, ideally you want a blue light to jolt you back to life.

Jono is the epitome of an ideas man — with friends he recently entered a raft built from Swiss balls and a volleyball net into a race on the Manawatu River. 'I always keep a pad up here — I've got to sketch ideas quickly before they go away.'

Completely solar-powered, the Skysphere is controlled by voice activations off Jono's phone. The phrase 'Doors open and lights on' brings the tower to life. His command of 'Beer please' receives a 'Coming right up' reply. Within seconds a can of lager magically appears from an arm-rest of the sofa. When stocks are running desperately low, an automated text message urgently requesting additional supplies gets sent to Jono's girlfriend, who lives in Palmerston North. It's possible to watch live sport in the Skysphere via a high-speed internet stream from Jono's father's Sky decoder situated down in the farmhouse.

'The sheep don't even know you're here,' he laughs. 'Hawks and kingfishers will glide past, oblivious to the tower.' The 'limousine tint' prevents birdlife from being able to see what's going on inside. 'The window is basically two pieces of polycarbonate, which made me consider expansion and contraction due to temperature. It shrinks more than steel. I think it grows about 40 millimetres, depending on temp and diameter. The seals allow movement. I found the equation on Google. I looked up the expansion of coefficients of different materials. All new to me. The reason I found out about all of this was after finding that I needed a rubber washer when drilling into steel. The rubber washer is to allow expansion and movement. I thought I'd better look into it. I love learning new stuff.

'I determined the height by sitting on the forks of a forklift. When I got to the point where it felt right (9 metres) I thought that would do. No need to get all silly about it. I did the height Health and Safety course. I was arguing with the lecturer about whether it's all gone too far, and he ended up agreeing with me. You would hit the ground from here at about 50 kilometres an hour,' says Jono, while our legs dangled over the edge. 'You've got a 33 per cent chance of surviving,' he states

matter-of-factly. 'It can wobble a bit here in the wind, but the tower is rated for an 8.5 earthquake. The main tube is 8 millimetres thick steel, and the whole structure weighs about 5.5 tonne, sitting on a 50-tonne pad.'

Jono admits he informed all of his family and friends about his Skysphere concept pre-construction. 'That didn't add any pressure at all. Telling everybody, that actually helped me finish it. You know, everyone was expecting me to do it. I probably didn't need to do that in hindsight, because I enjoyed the process. But as I posted progress photos, everyone was really supportive. The structure was assembled down on the flat, and a 30-tonne digger carved out a wide enough road, the 4-tonne Skysphere was towed uphill to its final resting place. 'The moment when I finally stood the tower up was pretty special.'

The young designer has since received literally hundreds of orders for his masterpiece to be duplicated. 'People want to throw money at me. But I'm so busy with my other work, I don't really have much spare time.' Nevertheless, Jono has already begun thinking about building a house … on wheels, of course.

Dave

THE OZONE

Hidden somewhere deep in Middle Earth, between creaking vines of bountiful crops, stands The Ozone, a creative hub for musicians, travellers and free-thinkers alike.

'I guess I'm a little bit of a hippy in my vibe,' reflects Dave, who for all intents and purposes could be called The Ozone's curator. 'I returned from living in a very open-minded, liberal community overseas, back to this very conservative area, and wondered "How am I going to keep my sanity?" Instead of going out and pissing all my money against the wall, I decided to create this space and bring the good times here.'

An old orchard packing shed has been meticulously converted into a vibrant recording studio. Walls and ceilings of bunker-like thickness have been soundproofed, transforming the structure's rigidity to bomb-shelter density.

Dave tries his best to give me a layman's crash-course into the science of soundproofing and insulation. 'The builder found it challenging,' he smiles, 'because nothing can be flush in a recording studio. Parallel walls bounce sound, hence the exterior layers of insulation to absorb, while the curved plywood panels reflect.'

The building's nondescript exterior cladding provides no clues whatsoever to passing trade as to what lies behind its heavily-padded walls. Once the portal-like door seals behind you, all traces of the sun's rays instantly dissipate, and LED lighting illuminates the melodic interior. One could easily be forgiven for thinking one has been transported to a Hollywood backroom or a Memphis studio.

A row of gleaming guitars are racked against one wall. 'What you see here is mostly vintage gear, with models dating from 1954 to 1982. I'm a bit of a tinkerer, and have restored a lot of equipment. These are all classic guitars: they are art. I can just sit there and look at them and think "Fuck, they're cool."

'While they are also collectable, and some of these guitars have turned out to be good investments, I never purchase them for that reason. When you follow your passion and your heart, you're following your truth anyway. As a result, you're going to make good decisions.

'The first real guitar I bought was off a mate for $250 in the late 1990s. It really was a piece of shit when I bought it — wires were hanging out, but it sounded really good. I gave it a complete overhaul and still play it today.'

Another distinctive-looking guitar catches my eye, prompting an enquiry into its pedigree. 'That's the holy grail of 12-strings,' Dave replies. 'A 1976 Guild F412. The very same model that The Eagles produced so much of their music on.'

Every item in Dave's music arsenal is functional, even the 1926 gramophone. 'If I don't use it, I lose it. The truth is I'm really going for tone.'

Dave's favourite genres are Rock'n'Roll and Blues, although he likes to infuse his own nuances. 'I have my own style, it can get pretty heavy, but I like that sound that I grew up with. You don't even have to be a musician to appreciate it. When you hear an Angus Young AC/DC power chord plugged into a Marshall — nothing else, no digital — that's Rock'n'Roll heaven. But you need certain gear to get that sound. That's what my collection is all about.'

Dave loves nothing better than inviting newcomers into The Ozone to listen, play or record. He regards music as the universal language. 'It doesn't matter if it's Classical or Death Metal. Turn your TV off, turn off your internet. Come down here, have a beer, have a laugh, and listen to some sounds. Leave here with a smile on your dial.

'I've been to a lot of amazing places, but to me life's still all about making connections with cool people. With all the neggo shit that we constantly have thrown at us, it's nice to be able to give something good back. After all,' he adds, 'we live in a criminal system that poses as free-market capitalism.'

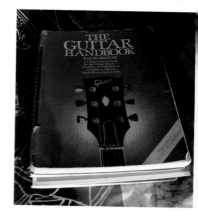

Dave is adamant that every living soul is both creative and inherently good. 'We've just got to find a way to bring it out. Humans are amazing. We really are, and possess a capacity for the infinite. I truly believe that.' For Dave, The Ozone is a hub, a meeting place where ideas can be shared and friendships made.

'The music industry is at a real crossroads. It's an interesting place right now. Musicians work so hard in the studio to produce an indefinable sound. But then their music goes out and is compressed. It just sounds like shit. They say music played on an MP3 has just 10 per cent of its original signal.

'The more you edit, while you may technically enhance, you also start to lose what's real. So why,' he enquires with refreshing foresight, 'don't we take this situation in a positive light? Let's bring back live music by getting people together and appreciating each other's company.'

When asked to comment on the essence of the Man Cave movement, Dave provides an enlightening response: 'I call it a relationship-saver. You've got to have space. I believe that my partner needs her space just as I need space. Ninety per cent of the time she knows that if I need my space, then this is where I will be. People just don't get that in life these days, but they need it. Even if it's just a little garage or a little corner.

'I've been a bit of a nomad, hippy traveller. So most of my life all I've really owned has been my backpack. I've had very few material possessions. I don't own a house or anything. To have a private space where I can shut the door and play my music is incredible.'

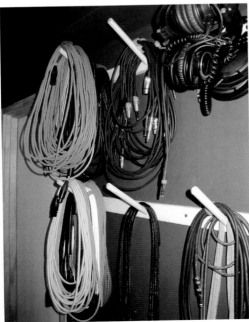

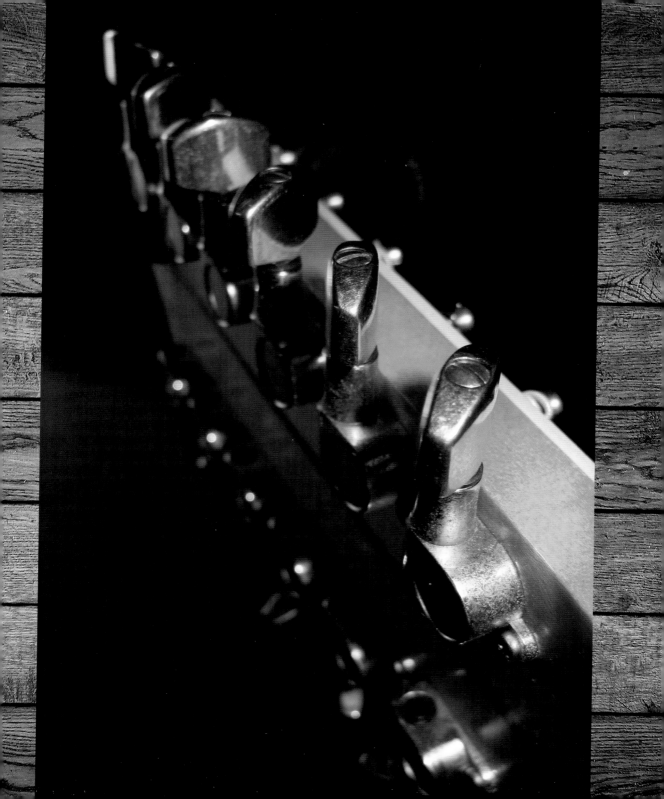

Skewered fish (or Fish-on-a-stick)

SERVES 3–4

500g thick fish fillet (salmon, kingfish, hapuku),
cut into 3cm cubes
1 red onion, peeled, quartered, separate layers
apart
2 capsicums, any colour, cut into 3cm dice
15 button mushrooms, cut in half

Marinade
250g soy sauce
125g mirin or sweet wine
125g water
100g brown sugar
1 clove of garlic, whole
a small slice of fresh ginger (optional)

10–12 x 25cm bamboo or metal skewers

To make the marinade, put all of the ingredients
in a small pot, bring to the boil, and turn the
heat down to simmer, reducing to a light syrup
consistency, approximately 15 minutes.

Soak the skewers in water for 15 minutes.

To make the skewers up, alternatively
thread on chunks of fish, onion, capsicum and
mushroom.

Brush with the marinade, and grill on a grill
plate or on the barbeque until tender.

Serve drizzled with the cooking marinade,
as a snack on its own, or with salad or rice for a
meal.

PAT'S PALACE

'I grew up around antiques and history. My grandparents were founding members of MOTAT in Auckland, and as far back as I can remember we went there for holidays and spent our days dressed in pioneer clothes and playing all over the place.

'Home always had loads of antiques and collectables throughout it, and we tended to live in 1900s villas. I still love those old houses, and would easily spend hours in a museum if my family allowed me! Times change and so do tastes, and with a more modern house the antiques and collectables can look out of place quickly.

'I suppose having a Man Cave is one of those "I want" things that husbands and dads often don't get a chance to do. After living in our current home for five years or so it was quite a spur-of-the-moment thing to turn an extra detached garage we had (storing junk) into something usable. It was during a tidy-up in the main garage that the pile of "things that can't get thrown away" started looking bigger than the things used, and so an idea was formed.

'What sparked the whole Man Cave idea was a pile of rusted corrugated iron sitting on the side of the road in central Whangarei, which had come from a garage that had been re-roofed. After I'd driven past it three times over two weeks, I thought, "Stuff it", went home, grabbed the trailer and loaded it up. From there, it just escalated — pallets, the rougher the better, were collected from industrial yards, any old scrap timber was assessed for use and taken home. Then, over a couple of weekends and a couple of late nights in winter, the modern Zincalume garage outside was transformed into a rustic shed inside.

'From there it was simply a case of arranging decades of old shit strategically. The "camping" fridge was moved down, a bar made up of old chests of drawers was built, a new lounge suite was bought for home, and the old one relegated. All of my rugby memorabilia was dragged out of boxes and organised — seriously, this took the longest time, as with each old programme, jersey, tie, pin, etc, a memory was stirred. Rugby stuff spanning 30-plus (and still counting) years of playing. Team sheets rekindling memories of games played and friendships made. At the time you tuck these things away after a game or season, you never really know why, but I'm glad I did so many times now — and glad my dad did as well, as he's contributed programmes from games he went to both before me and to watch me.

'I guess what I've got is a place where the history of an average Kiwi rugby player can be kept for him, his mates and his family to look at (and laugh at the old man probably). It's already growing the next generation with my son's first senior club jersey and tie joining the jerseys and ties from teams I played in or against.

'Along with the rugby memorabilia, there are plenty of other reminders of moments past. The tractors and some of the other kids' toys were built by my engineer grandfather for my mum and aunty, and have been thrashed by kids for decades — and will probably be dragged down at some stage for more. There's a little shrine to my father-in-law, Bill, who passed away a few years back. He would've loved a shed like this, too. The alcohol-related stuff comes from repping for liquor companies — I even have an ice bank to install one day and connect the taps up to. (It will be a long day when that happens — wouldn't want to leave a keg tapped and not drained!)

'We've got the internet connected down here. (The Cave is about 50 metres from the main house, heading into our paddock.) During the summer when our son is back from uni, I shift my office down here, so it's very convenient. It's a nice, quiet spot away from the house if anyone needs space or a chance to watch rugby without disruption — or watch rugby with total disruption.

'The next step is to finish off a platform outside, which will be a golf tee: just a spot to smack balls down into the bottom of the paddock or even sit out in the sun and enjoy an outside bevvie.

'I imagine that, like most Man Caves, it's never finished and never big enough. There's still more stuff to be installed somewhere, somehow, but for now I'm pretty content with how it looks and feels.'

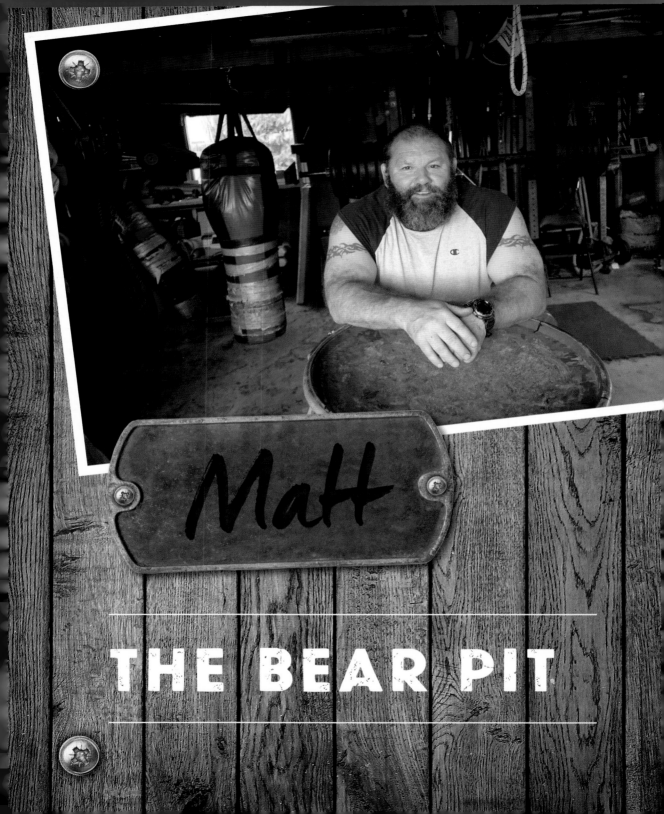

Matt

THE BEAR PIT

FOCUS YOUR MIND. BE POSITIVE, BE AGGRESSIVE. BACK YOURSELF. '

'No pain, no champagne!' roars former New Zealand powerlifter and strongman Matt. Despite being a shareholder in two commercial gyms, Matt prefers to train in the sanctuary of The Bear Pit, his Papamoa garage which contains over 2 tonnes of weights equipment.

'Getting strong isn't an overnight thing, it takes years under the bar. You've got to be willing to sacrifice. Anyone can get strong. But you've got to maintain it or you will become weak and pitiful.'

Matt offers a few words of wisdom for those wanting to develop their strength levels. 'Squatting parallel is always an interesting exercise for new lifters — they feel like they're going to explode. And you want to avoid people who get all their training tips off the internet.

'Behind every overnight sensation, there's a decade of work. And if you don't like that, then be happy with second or third. These days I train purely for enjoyment: if I feel like having a beer or going fishing instead, then that's what I do. A top athlete has to be obsessive-compulsive about their training. When I wore the silver fern, I trained six days a week.'

Shaun

THE BIKE &
BOVINE

During a stint living in Old Blighty with wife, Claire, and their four children, Shaun fell in love with the quintessential British public house. 'There's nothing like an English pub, with its low ceilings, horse tack and pewter mugs. They're not all about drinking to excess. I could spend an evening in a pub over there just sitting on one to two pints, but striking up conversation with all kinds of interesting people.'

Shaun admits becoming captivated by the UK pub life, complete with overfed Labradors dozing in corners, fires roaring in fireplaces, ploughman's lunches, pork scratchings, and a bell being rung for last orders to mark the end of play. This pub culture resonates with many Kiwis who have spent time in Britain's watering-holes, in stark contrast to the empty booze-barns and barren car parks that are still commonplace here in New Zealand.

Missing those delectable UK chocolate-box-style interiors, to which he had so become accustomed, Shaun set himself the mammoth task in 2005 of recreating a

Cotswolds pub in an old stable block on his property … albeit in the heart of rural Canterbury, New Zealand.

He admits that the devastation of the Christchurch earthquakes, which saw a number of watering-holes reduced to rubble, partly prompted his quest to create premises that his employees could socialise in together for their annual Christmas function. With great gusto, Shaun set himself a lofty goal of meticulously transforming the old stable block situated on his 10-acre lifestyle block property.

To create an authentic and believable English public house, he worked tirelessly, late into the middle of untold week nights, and throughout most weekends. His three-room pub, complete with a ladies lounge, a snug and a games room, nearly extracted every last ounce of energy, but he still managed to complete his project on time.

Shaun admits being so tired that he found the grand opening 'a bit of a blur'. The occasion, which doubled as his company's Christmas do, kicked off at 11am, with Shaun only having finally downed tools less than eight hours earlier. A crowd of 120 enthralled guests were treated to Hoppy Frog on tap that day, a beer brewed by several of Shaun's colleagues.

'The rules are pretty simple,' Shaun states. 'There's no TV in here, so it's all about the art of conversation. And it's about quality beer, not quantity. We have held special nights for the neighbours, too — everyone who lives on our road. It's so cool. Some of them had never met each other previously, and now we all get to know each other.'

Some of the neighbours have taken the arrangement one step further, seconding the bar to celebrate their own festivities. Shaun is more than happy to approve such requests. 'We've had birthdays in here, work functions, anniversaries and Christmas parties. The current capacity is 140.'

Much of The Bike & Bovine's interior was lugged and shipped back from the UK in boxes, bags and excess baggage carried by Shaun and his family. The contents originally were part of a sixteenth-century pub located somewhere in Warwickshire. The level of Shaun's craftsmanship and attention to detail has even tugged at the heartstrings of guests, prompting unexpected emotional reactions. 'We've had heaps of Brits in here,' explains Shaun, 'and they just love it. I found an English lady in the snug crying her eyes out once. She said the pub was so authentic it had made her homesick.'

Those amazing finishing chattels and attention to detail, including the Real Ale beer pumps, the black telephone, the scale-model sailing ship, the period newspapers of the day and the horse brasses, give Shaun's pub its ethereal quality. His seventeenth-century beer tankards originated from a Scottish manor house. The leather-bound books on display were legally acquired 40 years ago from a Central Otago gold fields court that Shaun was being paid to clean.

'When you step through the pub door, you are transported back into a 1940s traditional English country pub. Just magic,' says Shaun.

Since word has filtered around the traps, and various articles in the print media have been published extolling the virtues of The Bike & Bovine, Shaun has been forced to consider additional measures to protect its anonymity. 'We've had the odd unexpected visit from members of the public,' he concedes. 'Luckily, the pub sign is tucked well around the corner, obscured away from street view.'

Further expansion of The Bike & Bovine is on the cards: the addition of a microbrewery will be Shaun's next *pièce de résistance*, and is eagerly awaited by his friends and neighbours.

ON
THIS SITE
SEPT. 5, 1782
NOTHING
HAPPENED.

Kirsty
(ONE FOR THE LADIES)

THE BUS

'I think everyone loves an adventure and a bit of a story,' reflects Kirsty, while pouring out a glass of wine aboard The Bus, which is currently positioned down the back of their Mount Base vineyard.

'Initially, I was looking at either a Portacom or a caravan for us to use as a staff-, meeting- and entertainment-type space, but windows and open space are very important to me, and everything I looked at felt small and enclosed. Then I found the bus, a Bedford 500 Diesel with a mid-mounted engine.

'It was originally one of the Mount Cook fleet. I've got some of the old logbooks, which is cool. We have turned them into a visitors book now.' The iconic Mount Cook Group was founded by New Zealand transport and tourism operator Rodolph Wigley in 1912.

'I found the bus in Waihi: the owner and his wife had spent 18 months travelling around New Zealand in it. All of my friends thought I was crazy buying a bus, but

that usually only encourages me more. My dad and his mate, Mark, who has a bus-driving licence, set off on a roadie back down south to Marlborough in it for me.

'My parents,' Kirsty laughs, 'in a moment of weakness, offered to strip the bus out and refit the interior.' After assessing the vehicle's condition upon arrival, Kirsty's mother seemed to have second thoughts. 'She looked at me and asked, "What have you done?" I didn't really have time to answer, as my bags were packed and I was on my way to Bali for two weeks — I still get in trouble for that one.'

A major refurbishment ensued. Hearty, honest graft has transformed the old bus into something rather unique. It has a comfy lounge, designed so you can sit back and watch the sun setting through a wall of windows. It has also been designed to transform into a getaway apartment for Kirsty on occasion.

The bus has been fitted out with a fireplace, an oven and a fridge; 'a wineglass dishwasher might be next,' she laughs.

An existing solar panel on the roof charges four house batteries, which power the lights, water pumps and stereo. 'An auto-electrician wired 10 of the 12 original speakers back to life. We play music through Pandora on my iPod. The sound is actually incredible.'

A major refurbishment of the bus's exterior has been undertaken by Kirsty over the past year. Sandpaper, scrapers, rollers and elbow grease have given the old luxury liner a much-needed facelift; its decaying façade, patched up and lovingly given a coat of vibrant green sheen. 'I love working away on her when I can, as not only is it satisfying to see the improvements, but I find it's a great thinking space in a busy life.'

A barbeque has been fitted into one of the exterior compartments where luggage was once stowed.

'We've also built an external toilet, including a porcelain basin plumbed in with old taps, and a lavender-lined stone pathway leading to the outdoor shower. My colleague Ross and I built a movable deck; I was his lackey, doing what I was told and nailing everything down.'

The bus has quickly become a much-loved addition to the Mount Base landscape for Kirsty's staff, colleagues and friends. She has fresh-baked focaccia bread on the table, beside it sits a pear chutney made with pears from their neighbour's tree, a lamb roast is in the oven, covered in a Merlot sauce made that morning, and, of course, a chilled bottle of their Sauvignon Blanc awaits. 'We actually try really hard to keep the vineyard as natural as possible. We have lots of wildlife around, including pheasants, quail, hawks and a native falcon. Plus we have sheep to keep the weeds down, and are currently planting more native trees. There's a real emphasis on maintaining biodiversity, using wild flowers and insect life to keep everything as naturally balanced as possible.

'Stripping the old bus out and turning it into a bar has made for wonderful entertaining. Being able to drive her around the vineyard and park up in different spots to watch the sun go down is such a treat. The beauty of the vista here is breathtaking, so to sit back with a drink in hand after a good day's work and enjoy the moment is priceless. I love character and history. This has all the elements. I'm just so chuffed that we actually pulled this idea off and it works so well! Now for the next idea ...'

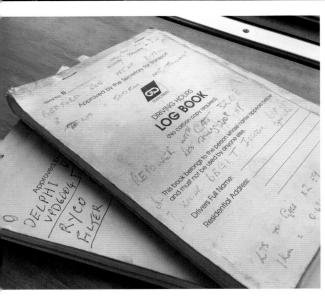

Terry

MUNRO'S SHED

'We moved to this property nine years ago, and a big Man Cave was always the plan,' Terry admits. 'I've always had elements of hoarding in my blood,' laughs the Christchurch resident. 'Being born and bred on the farm, you learn never to throw anything away.' A major shed-build ensued, with Terry playing a leading hand in all aspects of the project, including working on the wiring, plumbing and laying the concrete base. Multi-vehicle garaging aside, the current structure also includes office, bar, kitchen and theatre. An additional 26 square metre extension is in the pipeline. Terry intends to add dental-, tobacconist- and dairy-themed rooms. 'I need more space to take the pressure off the shed,' he smiles.

'I do get a real thrill when sharing my collection with others. Most people who come around here understand it. Except my sister-in-law.' He laughs. 'She just can't get her head around it. I regularly have bike and car clubs here doing shed runs, and we often get the barbeque out for them.

'My biggest passion since the age of seven years old has been '57 Chevs. Even though my dad had Studebakers and DeSotos, it was my uncle's '57 that I loved the most. I couldn't afford one in my teens or twenties.'

Much later in life, when Terry found himself in a position to purchase his dream car, Carol, his wife of 30 years, was completely supportive, knowing exactly how much the iconic '57 Chev meant to her husband. Terry admits the thrill of the chase was enormous. He ended up with not one, but two, '57s. 'Initially, I planned to import both cars and then sell one to pay for the other. As it turned out I decided to keep both. I've got the biggest collection of '57 Chev memorabilia in New Zealand. At one stage, I had 10 boxes a day arriving at my door!'

Terry's most prized personal possession would be his father's bronze 1973 Valiant Ranger. 'I remember Dad dropping me off in the car: it was a Tuesday morning and I was on my way to a school camp. He passed away soon after, and I never saw him again. I was 12 years old.'

The car has remained with the family ever since. 'Mum never drove or sat her licence. She had a boarder from 1973 to 1995 who drove her everywhere. When I finally got the car, in 1994 or 1995, the registration had lapsed, with just 73,000 kilometres on the clock. It's still like new, and today the odometer reads 83,000. I took her down to Twizel recently, and she still sits so well on the road.'

Another iconic vehicle parked up nearby is the 1946 Merc convertible, which comes from New York but was purchased in New Zealand. 'With just two owners and 35,000 miles on the clock, it was a pretty special car to find,' Terry admits. 'I just love the States, it's like a second home.' In 2015, Terry undertook a nine-week

vacation, covering 11,000 miles and 19 states. 'I returned home with 39 boxes of collectables. Hence the need for extending the shed! I collect everything, not just petrol-related stuff. For me, it's about preserving history and leaving something for my children.'

Terry has one iconic national treasure on display in his shed: a trailer built from an old Indian sidecar. 'What Burt Munro achieved was absolutely incredible,' reflects Terry. 'He first went to Bonneville in 1959 as a spectator, and decided then and there that he would return and compete.' Munro spent nearly a decade racing on the famed Salt Flats, setting world records in 1962, 1966 and 1967. He was still racing at Bonneville in 1971, well into his seventieth year.

'I found the trailer completely by accident,' explains Terry. 'While searching '57 Chev stuff on eBay, I found and purchased a 1964 copy of *Mechanix Illustrated* magazine, which I had been told had been mentioned in *The World's Fastest Indian* movie. That got me wondering what other Burt Munro memorabilia was around. Lo and behold, I found a Burt Munro bike trailer for sale on eBay. I researched it thoroughly: my wife, who worked at Technical Books at the time, brought a few books home containing photos, which I used to compare with the item on sale. I soon realised that the eBay item was an original.'

Bidding at that stage was restricted to American eBay members only; however, an impassioned plea by Terry convinced the seller to let him join the auction. 'He actually sent me additional original photos of Burt and the trailer. I was the only person outside of America given permission to bid.'

It's fair to say that several state-side collectors were incensed about Terry's late inclusion, with the seller receiving several threatening phone messages. Terry moved quickly to ensure that the trailer could be shipped back to New Zealand before anything untoward happened to the iconic artefact.

To this day, the figure Terry paid remains a secret. When pushed, he admits that it was a little higher than he had intended, but later realised he was in possession of the world's most famous motorbike trailer.

'The last time Burt used the trailer was in 1971, during a documentary filmed by Roger Donaldson, and the axle actually snapped, as portrayed in the movie. You can see where it was welded up and reinforced by a piece of flat steel.'

Because the trailer's New Zealand number plate (attached in true Kiwi fashion with number-six wire and PK screws) was yellow, like Californian plates were at the time, Munro towed his famous bike illegally around the States under the noses of local law enforcement for nearly a decade.

'I never got to meet Burt, but as a V8-loving teenager from Invercargill who was into drag racing at Teretonga in the 1970s, I had heard about him. However, I don't really think at that stage many New Zealanders truly appreciated what this incredible man really achieved.'

Terry's long-term goal is to sell the trailer to a Munro enthusiast from Invercargill, returning this iconic piece of New Zealand history to the deep south, back where it belongs. Another option would be to sell it to Te Papa or a similar museum, where it can be appreciated by all.

THE
MOSSBURN
MOB OF
LONERS

'I learnt to shoot here, so did my brothers. We learnt to respect guns, and also had a lot of fun. The pond was built in 1976, one year before I was born,' recalls Muzz, 'on Allan Turner's farm; he was best mates with my dad.

'Dad and Allan used to shoot at a little pond about 800 metres higher up the gully. They had this idea for a long time, to build a bigger pond in the swamp lower down.' The pair finally got the green light after Allan received a Catchment Acclimatisation Grant. 'The new pond was perfect, right under a flight path. After a lot of work had been carried out to prepare the site, there was a major setback when heavy rain eroded the bank, draining it completely and forcing Dad and Allan to head back up the gully for one more season.

'I remember another year there had been a fair bit of rain and the creek flooded. You had to cross this little bridge to get to the maimai, and my brother was bowled over while crossing it by an over-excited Labrador who ran between his legs. He was fished out of the drink about 20 metres downstream. Dad missed the first hour of shooting because he had to take my brother home.

'When I came back from the UK, 10 years ago, we contacted the new owner of the farm to ask for permission to shoot the pond again. He was more than happy for us to return, so long as we respected the place. We really appreciate and respect the fact that he was good enough to let us back in.

'The old hut, which was the sleep-out, had been moved under the block of pine trees that my dad and Allan had planted. Someone had made a half-arsed attempt

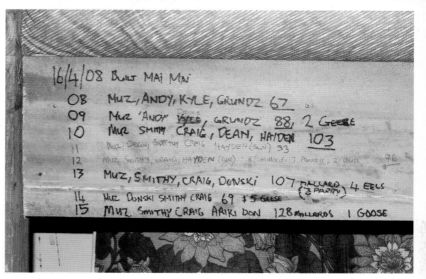

to turn it into a maimai. We've since added an 8 metre by 8 metre extension to it over the pond, and built the lounge/kitchen area.'

The 'team' comprise two builders, a sparkie and an engineer. Muzz swears it's a fluke that the three blokes he shoots with all happen to possess complementary skills. 'They certainly weren't handpicked just to work on the maimai,' he laughs.

The Friday before opening day is a huge event in itself for the boys. 'Everyone's bloody excited — this year, Smithy was just fizzing, mate. Donny's brother, who is a lawyer in Sydney, flies over especially for opening weekend and supplies the port! We head out to the maimai in the morning for last-minute preparations. This year we held a golf tournament in the afternoon, all of us dressed as English gentlemen. The clubs we used were from the 1970s — the same age as the pond.'

The boys play golf for the 'Mob of Loners' trophy, in reference to an interesting turn of phrase coined while the boys were shooting one memorable afternoon. 'You always get that lone duck flying overhead,' says Muzz, 'commonly called "the loner". One of the boys spotted a pair of ducks flying past and said there was a "mob of loners" coming in. The term has stuck ever since.'

The pond itself is in good health; in fact, bird numbers are soaring (pardon the pun). 'In Dad's day it was standard to chop 100 ducks during opening weekend. When we started shooting here again, we only bagged 67 in the first year, and a not much better 88, 12 months later. But we shot 128 ducks last year during opening weekend, and 138 this year, plus 15 Canadian geese. Clear blue skies, sun out and a gentle breeze blowing down the valley. Perfect conditions for this place.

'Our wives and girlfriends know the place is perfect, but we always find additional improvements. We've held four working-bee weekends here since late January.' Muzz built the self-feeder from an old washing-machine, set up on an island in the middle of the pond. 'I cut the bottom out, left a gap about an inch wide, and fitted a tray underneath which the ducks feed off. So we just fill the barrel full of grain and leave them to it.'

The maimai contains life's essential elements, as well as the odd luxury; running water in the form of a full 20-litre bucket stationed on the shelf above the sink, and cable TV. 'There's a small hose attached to the container so we can wash our hands or have a drink. We also hook up the laptop, type in the password and connect to Sky,' reveals Muzz, 'so we can watch the Super 18 rugby on Friday night.

'I just love it here — everything about it, actually. We're set up on the opposite side of the pond from my dad's old maimai. We return for the roar as well, when we hunt a block up the Takitimus together. This place means so much; it's just like a house to me.'

GUY'S ROAST DUCK RECIPE

1 mallard duck (preferably head-shot, which saves any metal-detecting by guests upon eating)

1 small brown onion, diced

1 Tbsp dried sage (add more if you prefer a stronger flavour)

2 cups fresh breadcrumbs

salt and pepper to taste

1 small egg, beaten

a scoop of dripping

1 cup water, and a wee glug of red wine (optional)

cornflour

chicken or vegetable stock, if required

Pluck the feathers of the bird, and remove its entrails.

Preheat the oven to 150°C.

Wash the duck, and pat it dry, inside and out.

To make the stuffing, add the onion, sage, breadcrumbs and seasoning to the beaten egg, and mix well.

Stuff the duck and place it in a lidded roasting dish (no roasting bag required), with the dripping, water and wine.

Cook in the oven for 60–90 minutes, depending on your oven. (Long, slow cooking gives the best results.)

Whip up your gravy from the pan drippings. Add cornflour to thicken. If there is insufficient moisture in the pan, use either a chicken stock or a vegetable stock to give it a boost.

Serve the bird with your favourite roast vegetables, greens and at least one glass of beer. Enjoy!

THE DUKE
OF EARL

LION BROWN

RANFURLY SHIELD

WELLINGTON 1982

BREWED & BOTTLED BY LION BREWERIES LTD WELLINGTON / 745ml

'A mate of mine, called Earl, actually did all the wiring in here when I decided to get this place up and running. We both loved the song "Duke of Earl" [by Gene Chandler], so it was an easy choice to name the bar,' says Craig.

Despite residing in Christchurch for the past 33 years, Craig has remained a staunch Stokes Valley Wellingtonian. 'Being down here in Red and Black country for so long probably was a real incentive to start a Wellington, Hurricanes and Lion Brown collection. I used to have a heap of *Star Wars* memorabilia as well, but I sold all that. It's good to specialise in one genre.'

The Duke of Earl is the Christchurch branch headquarters of the Wellington Rugby Supporters club. 'We've had 50 in here before, but there's probably 15 diehards. "Missionaries amongst the heathens" is how we describe ourselves,' he laughs. 'Club members meet here before every game, even when the Canes are playing in South Africa. We will watch the footy, then fire up the barbeque outside for breakfast.

'Christian Cullen, the Paekakariki Express, is actually our patron. There's a framed photo of Cully and I hanging on the wall over there. Christian hasn't actually visited here yet — it's about time he did. We would love to host him.'

The Duke of Earl copped a bit of damage during the Christchurch earthquakes: 'I lost two dozen bottles of red wine, some of my Lion Brown, and several glass frames were smashed. Everything's been fully repaired or replaced now, though.'

The 1982 Lion Brown Wellington Ranfurly Shield bottle is Craig's favourite memento. 'It's never been opened and never will. Would taste like vinegar now anyway. I found the bottle on Trade Me two or three years ago. Lion Brown was always the locals' beer of choice, growing up in Wellington. Trade Me is a great source for collectors. I just picked up a Lion Brown Light for $146.

'I've got a full set of twizzle sticks with international rugby motifs. They're made of metal and heavy. I've still got the original black envelope packaging. When the set arrived, I noticed New Zealand was missing, so I rang the lady, who found it. She apologised and posted it straight down.

'It's funny, because even some of the members who come here all the time, they ask me when I acquired various items. I've had some of the stuff for years; because there are so many things in here, even regulars haven't seen them before.

'It's taken me 12 years to get the Duke of Earl to the stage that I'm really happy with it. All I wanted initially was a fridge, a dart board and an armchair.

DUKE of EARL

'Finding and collecting old pieces of memorabilia involves meaning and history. Buying new stuff is too sterile for my liking: I want my place to have heart. That's really important to me.

'I've got an old sign from the Waterloo Hotel in Wellington hanging outside. When it's time for a beer, I also put up a Lion Brown placard. My mates drive past and see the signal. It's like attracting moths to a flame.'

Footnote: The answer is 'yes', for those readers who are wondering whether Captain Hurricane himself has ever visited the Duke of Earl.

Dan

FACIAL HAIR ETIQUETTE

'The most annoying thing about having a beard are the number of window-lickers continually wanting know when I'm going to be shaving it off,' says Dan, the owner of a magnificent bushy ginga beard. 'It's also a complete myth that food gets stuck in your beard,' he divulges. 'Maybe the odd crumbly remnant of a potato chip may get caught, but to be honest I love my food too much to store any on my face.

'I went to the Somersault music festival once, near Barnstaple, and a photographer approached my girlfriend, Rosie, to see if he could take a pic. Rosie quickly did her hair and makeup, but then the guy apologised and said he actually only wanted to take *my* photo. He was doing a portfolio on beards. If you Google "David Oakwood photography" and search for beards, you will find me along with many other fine manly specimens.

'I did shave my beard off once, after the last game of the season, without telling my girlfriend. I went home after the game, had a quick shave, shower, got changed and went out on the town for a few pints. My mates couldn't believe I'd parted with my trademark beard. Early the next morning, I went around to her house and banged on the door. She opened the door, took one look at me and slammed the door shut. Rosie didn't even recognise me!' he roars.

'I did have a clump of beard pulled out one time during a fight playing rugby. It looked like a bit of a mess, and I did debate shaving it off again. But I just let it be, and within no time at all my mane was restored back to full volume.'

Dan disagrees with the notion that bushy beards get prickly in the peak of summer. 'That's the other question everyone always asks. To be honest, I'm fully acclimatised to beard life. It feels the same as when I was clean-shaven.

'I never ever trim my beard for length or thickness, but every few months a mate who is a barber might fade the sideburns next to my ears. I don't use beard oil, I use organic coconut oil. I keep a tub of it on top of my toolbox at work. My facial hair gets so thick that it's like [rusty — he's a ranga] wire wool. Here's a tip for you,' he reveals. 'I tend to use my fingers as opposed to a brush, because the brush tends to rip my hair out.'

Matt

HOP TIPS

'An economics teacher at school used to tell us that, such were the restrictions on hop- and tobacco-growing in New Zealand, the government knew just how many plants there were and where each one of them was. That wasn't quite the reality, but there were times when getting hops for home-brewing was harder than walking into the Fiordland bush and seeing a moose.

'A story told in my family is of a great-uncle up north who, decades ago, liked to brew his own beer. He had some precious hops drying in a shed when a tornado swept through town. Roofing iron was taken clean off the shed, and the hops were blown away. Naturally, his first concern was to recover the lost hops.

'His nephew, an expert brewer for many years, once told me that when he couldn't get hold of hops he tried using kumarahou (gumdigger's soap) leaves in a mix. "What did it taste like?" I asked. He replied, "Kumarahou."

'Like most urban backyard brewers, I only have space to grow enough hops to flavour a batch or two of beer each year, but the plants are a real talking point with visitors. If you've seen them commercially grown, they are trained onto tall poles. I ran mine along a fence, south to north.

'Pre-spring planting, the soil needs to be rich in organic matter, and then, once the hops are in, they need regular, deep watering.

'When the first runners appear, about the width of a pencil, cut them off. Don't worry: other runners will quickly appear, and you'll get a better crop production.

'Hops grow *fast*. They make bamboo look slow and lazy. Bullet hops are so named because of the speed at which they grow …

'Cones (flowers) drop from the runners in late summer. Before harvesting, let them dry to the point where they feel like origami paper. Then hang them in a warm, dry place in a breathable bag, giving it a shake-up every few days, to properly dry. Add a handful to a lager brew for bitterness once the fermentation has stopped.

'You can make hop tea, too, but be careful as it can be potent. The wife of a mate makes him a cup whenever he is planning on doing some "unnecessary" DIY. She swears it can make him sleep right through a long weekend.'

Stu

PIGS OF
THE 309

Stu doesn't have a favourite — he has 65 to 70 of them. 'I could never eat any of them, they're my friends,' says the likeable Coromandel icon. 'They don't argue with you, are extremely considerate and very clean.' All of Stu's mob sleep inside at night, either in his crib, shed or caravan. 'I built a pig flap so that they can pop out to the toilet. They're quite happy to lie with me in front of the heater during winters, and park up around the television. The Captain Cookers are a great breed. They're actually of French origin, not British, as most people assume.'

Whenever tourists pull over on Coromandel's 309 Road, which bisects Stu's farm, pigs coming running from all directions in search of a tasty morsel. It's not unusual to find boars or sows fast asleep on the metal road during the middle of the day, unfazed by passing traffic, logging trucks included!

Excited holidaymakers leave the safety of their vehicles to interact with Stu's pigs, which are so tame that they can be hand-fed, and the boars are quite partial to a tummy-rub from complete strangers. Securing one's vehicle is safe practice before interacting with the personable porkers, which have been known to propel themselves into vehicles, in scavenging mode. An English family found to their dismay that one offender had actually swallowed their car keys. 'I had a good idea which one swallowed them,' says Stu, matter-of-factly. 'So all we could do was wait for the keys to pass through the pig. The keys eventually turned up in a nearby paddock, covered in a bit of shit.'

The humble farmer is clearly thrilled about being continually bombarded by curious visitors to his rustic property. 'I feel so lucky to meet so many wonderful people. All animal-lovers, they wouldn't stop here otherwise.' Unfortunately, criminals regularly sneak onto Stu's block to slay his tame pigs. Naturally, Stu is devastated with each loss. He has also found pigs of his seriously wounded after being stabbed and then set upon by dogs.

Stu's bare feet are as much a topic of conversation as his pet pigs. 'I do wear shoes to funerals,' he concedes, 'but that's about it. I get a lot of funny looks when I go to places like Pukekohe for pig-meal. Or the time I went to Australia on holiday. I just feel comfortable being in bare feet on the farm; they really toughen up during summer.'

Rabbi

' THE TIMBER INSIDE THE
SHED CAME FROM MY
OLD PIG PENS. YOU CAN
STILL SEE THE MARKS
WHERE THE PIGS USED
TO SCRATCH AWAY.
I CAN'T REALLY TELL YOU
WHAT'S GONE ON INSIDE
HERE: IT'S JUST BLOODY
LUCKY THAT NONE OF
THESE WALLS CAN TALK. '

Paul

SMOKO WITH
THE AXEMAN

'We're on a fitness buzz, as you can see. To be fair, my body is probably more a like warehouse than a temple. "Temple of Doom",' laughs The Axeman.

'No fizzy drinks or processed crap around here.' However, the packet of chocolate chippies and the jellybean jar give the lie to his healthy-eating mantra. 'A body like this has got to get fed with pretty good tucker, mate, not pies and sugar.'

Turkish Delights and Cherry Heaven are the only morsels left in an open box of Roses chocolates. 'You do wonder why the chocolate people bother to make those flavours.' He makes a valid point: they're left untouched in every box of Roses in the country.

He winces upon recalling the time he smoked some fish for lunch in the workshop. 'I finally realised that all the burnt paper with the petrol and oil in it covering my bench top had evaporated into the fish. People were coming in all day grabbing a fork and having a bite. I don't smoke fish here anymore,' he admits ruefully.

The cluttered smoko room has been decorated in a random yet possibly eclectic style. An intriguing collection of brass military badges sits on the sill below heavily-barred windows. 'I found them in a box: they look like paratroopers' regalia, but I can't actually remember where I got the box from. One of my son's ex-girlfriends bought the butterfly on the wall for me when I was recovering in hospital after falling off me motorbike. I've also kept all of the steel work that came out of my leg, including all 15 screws, which were 6 millimetres long.'

A grand total of nine out-of-date calendars have been tacked to the walls; five display iconic black-and-white logging images, three promote women's swimsuits, and there is a barely used Collins 2015 Year Planner. 'I really just like looking at the pictures,' he confesses.

Paul services steel teeth for a living. 'I actually learnt to sharpen chainsaws in what was called the Sahara forest, now it's the desert of course.'

While the energetic bald-headed mechanic loves the vast majority of his customers, some clearly get his goat. Briggs & Stratton is an engine, not a type of lawn-mower. 'I don't know how many old guys come in demanding I find them a Briggs & Stratton blade. There's no such thing. The worst ones are old guys who may have once worked in the industry — you know, engineers or bulldozer mechanics. They always come in to kick tyres. They're retired, bored and have nothing to do at home. These guys always want things that I have no need to stock. They seem to think the parts they seek are common. In reality, they probably haven't been since the end of World War Two. Then, when I end up ordering parts for them, all they want to do is haggle the price.'

Ben

SHARP
SHOOTER

Electrician by day and snooker champion the rest of the time, an adolescent Ben spent a fair amount of his daytime hours honing his craft in the public houses of Oxford. 'These old places would be full of smoke: it may have been bad for your health, but it made for a great atmosphere. There were always deals going on around you — you know what I mean, men doing business. I was in there regularly playing snooker from about the age of 13 or 14.

'We used to go to a snooker club and play a game called Golf with lots of old fellas. You'd put a bit of dough in and head around the table, potting balls in different holes for various points. That game was good for developing skill. We were all playing for money, and as a young fella I didn't have too much of it, so you would always put that extra concentration in because you didn't want to lose it.

'There was another game where they'd put an ashtray on the middle of the pool table; there would be heaps of guys playing. Everyone would chuck £2 on the tray. You'd break, and if any ball hit the ashtray, 50 pence would get put straight in. You got 15 to 20 blokes all putting two points in there and taking turns — it adds up to a fair amount of money. The game was called Killer. You would have three lives; everyone's names would be put up on the board. You miss a shot and you'd lose a life. Then the next guy would have his turn.

'There was one other rule: if anyone's ball smashed the ashtray, that geezer copped an instant five-quid fine. It happened more than you would expect, with guys who'd had one pint too many getting frustrated and losing their rag.

'Everyone was always trying to stitch each other up. It's a prick of a game, but it certainly sharpened my skills, and made me grow up real fast as well.'

Mince on fried pasta

SERVES 6

Mince topping
2 tbsp olive oil
1 onion, roughly chopped
2 cloves of garlic, chopped or grated
4 rashers bacon, chopped
1 tsp dried thyme
1kg beef mince
2 x 400g tin chopped tomatoes
2 tbsp (squirts) of your favourite tomato sauce
200g button mushrooms, roughly chopped
1 tsp chilli flakes (optional)
a squirt of Worcestershire sauce

2 tsp sea salt
a few twists of freshly ground black pepper
a handful of fresh parsley, chopped

250g noodles, Italian or Asian, fresh or dried (eg, tagliatelle, pappardelle, udon) (use cooked leftovers if you have any lurking in the fridge)
a generous drizzle of olive oil for frying
sea salt and freshly ground black pepper
6 eggs
a handful of grated Cheddar cheese, to sprinkle on top

Heat the olive oil in a large, deep pan over a medium heat, and cook the onion, garlic, bacon and thyme for few minutes until soft. Add the mince, occasionally stirring for about 3–4 minutes until lightly coloured. Add everything else in the mince topping, and simmer for 25 minutes, until thick and tasty. Adjust the seasoning to taste.

Meanwhile, if not using leftover cooked noodles, cook the noodles according to the instructions on the packet. Drain them off and put them near the heat where you are cooking the mince, to dry off.

When the mince is ready, heat a drizzle of olive oil in a large pan and add the pasta, seasoning it and tossing it about a bit. Then spread it out and allow it to fry, until going crispy on the bottom and around the edges. While this is crisping, fry off the eggs.

To assemble, take the pasta pan off the heat; pile on the mince, sprinkle over the cheese, and serve topped with fried eggs.

HEAVY
INSULATED

'Have you fondled an insulator today?' laughs Jeff, a former wreck-diver and treasure-hunter, now a collector of electrical insulators. 'To be honest, it's getting hard to find something new. The challenge is to locate that next one. If you keep your eyes open, there's always stuff to be found.'

Jeff collects New Zealand-made insulators, or insulators that were exported for use here. He literally has thousands of them in his house, lining his garage and hanging all over his property. 'You've got your various makers, a lot of French stuff was actually sent to New Zealand.

'I don't like the idea of keeping boxes of stuff just stashed away: I put my stuff out to be seen. And if I can't display it, I will flick it off to someone else who wants it. There's no point having stuff hidden.

'I guess I've been a collector all my life. When I got back from Aussie in '94, I saw a few insulators lying around at my brother's place on the farm. I'd been aware of them before, of course, but just thought, "Hang on, they're quite nice." So I've just kept grabbing them. They're a cheap collectable.

'I used to go down to the old power depots and knock on the door. That's

all been kicked in the arse now with OSH, of course. They don't like you having accidents on their account anymore.'

Jeff has cleverly mounted and hung his enormous collection of insulators on old wooden power poles. 'I found out about an old pole lying on a rural block near Waihi. We dragged it out of the bush, on a bit of a pine forest, actually. Hauled it out by tractor, then cut it up and trailered her back home,' recalls Jeff, while leaning on the ship's anchor which has become a permanent feature on his back lawn.

'It is interesting to gauge visitors' reactions when they come here. Once the insulators are hung and displayed, you don't need to do a thing to them. The cobwebs might grow, but the rain cleans them up a bit. People do ask why I've bothered to collect all these things. My standard reply is always that some dork's got to do it!

'Two of us did a tour of the South Island in search of insulators. We took a mate's company car, bought a trailer in Christchurch, and returned with 14 triple-shed power pieces from the old Lake Coleridge line. I'm off to Invercargill next: I can't wait to see what I'm going to find down there.'

CLIMBING
PAST HERE WHILE LINE ALIVE
PROHIBITED

DANGER
WIRES

BEWARE
OF
FEED BACK

DANGER
11,000 VOLT
CABLE

DANGER
11,000 VOLT
CABLE
UNDERGROUND
IN VICINITY

DANGER
MEN WORKING
ON LINE

WARNING
BURIED
TELEPHONE
CABLES

INQUIRE
POST OFFICE
BEFORE
EXCAVATING

LIVE
WIRES

BEWARE

ILO

ver you go.

Goose

THE FOUR KINGS SHEEP BAA

'They were my lucky undies,' explains Goose, when asked about the pair of fraying and decrepit gruts framed alongside his last playing jersey. 'I wore them every game from my First XV days at Morrinsville College,' says Goose, who stopped playing premier rugby at the age of 33. 'They had to be blue because I was a St Joseph's man. My wife, Adele, used to hate them — she threatened to throw them out many times. I told her not to, because in the back of my mind I always had a special place for them.

'I remember going into the Pounamu Motor Inn years ago on a Marist team trip, and there the All Black front row's undies from the 1987 World Cup Final were framed on the wall. For some reason that image struck a chord.' Goose's garment does not come out of the frame for special occasions: 'they're extremely fragile'.

A pair of Goose's old footy boots sit on top of his homemade frame, constructed from ply, recycled timber and glass. 'The glass came from the four windows that used to run along this wall next to my bench top, before I ripped it out and put the French doors in. The toilet is going into the small room off the bar, into the laundry which Adele has been asking I get on with. I'm a bit of a perfectionist, though — I don't like to rush things,' he grins.

Goose spent many week nights during summer converting a section of his

garage into the Four Kings. 'Especially during daylight savings, the wife pretty much forgot what I looked like. It would be straight home after work and into the garage. I was working towards a May deadline; I didn't think it would be finished on time, but I gave it a real nudge.

'I would come home at night, occasionally with the ute loaded up with recycled timber. If during the day I was passing a derelict old house or shed in the country, I would rock in and ask the farmer or land owner if I could take some of the timber.'

The eye-catching internal cladding of the feature wall includes a variety of different-coloured and -textured boards, which Goose has cut to various lengths and applied a light sand to. The couches are made from pallets and an old mattress, two of which are long enough to stretch out and sleep on.

'Everyone loves the fridge, with its secret front door. It actually came from the local op shop. People say it needs to be sanded back and repainted, but I love it the way it is.

'The name, Four Kings Sheep Baa, is a bit of a play on words. We spent three weeks in Hong Kong, where they have all sorts of street names which sound a bit rude to foreigners. So I decided to follow suit with my bar. If you say "Four Kings Sheep" in a Benny Hill accent, it becomes instantly apparent.'

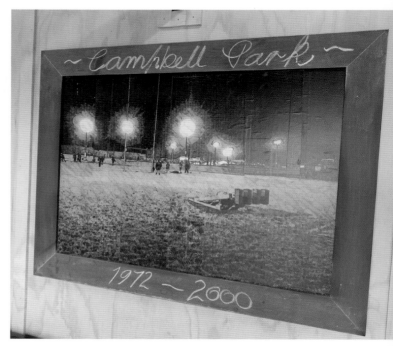

THE
FOUR KINGS

SHEEP
BAA

MAN
CAVE

GIRLS
STAY OUT
AS YOU SMELL

Potato chip chook

SERVES 6

6 skinless chicken breasts
200g butter, softened
2 large cloves of garlic, roughly chopped or grated
freshly ground black pepper
½ tsp dried tarragon (and/or a small bunch of fresh parsley, chopped)
1 large bag of potato chips (flavour of your choice)

Preheat the oven to 190°C, or fire up the barbeque.

Grease a baking dish large enough to contain the breasts in a single layer. Mix everything else together in a food processor, or just smash it all together in a bowl, to a crunchy peanut butter consistency. Slather it over the breasts and bake in the oven for 20 minutes. Alternatively, if you are using the barbeque, cook it with the lid down for about 30 minutes (until, when stabbed with a knife, the chicken juices run clear).

Chef's tip
The supermarket seems to sell the breasts of chickens that either are abusing steroids or think they are turkeys. I used a three-pack of these massive breasts and just cut them in half.

THE CLOG
AND BULL

'We used to go down to the Wellington Sevens, until one year when the tournament became really popular and the tickets sold out in about five minutes. I missed out, so decided to do something about it. We would hold the Sevens here instead,' says Tiss. 'So we set to work, building The Clog and Bull in one of the garages under the house.' The project went right down to the wire. 'Even on the first day of the Sevens, while we had a crowd here, the electrician was still wiring in the data projector. He finished about five minutes before New Zealand's opening first game.

'There's a few pairs of clogs on display down here. I've got my mum's old ones — my uncle actually used to make them in Holland,' says Tiss, while wearing an enormous yellow pair, which he happily worked in outside while living in the

Netherlands. Tiss reckons clogs are comfortable so long as you walk with your toes pointed up, otherwise the tops of your feet can rub a bit and lose a bit of bark.

Tiss has also set up an office in his Man Cave. 'I don't mind a bit of noise when I work,' he explains. 'I don't really get distracted, not when there's things you've got to get done. Every now and then I might take a break and watch a bit of rugby.

'My son and his mates often take over the place in the weekends, and that's what it's for. I sometimes come down here on Sunday mornings and find a few of the boys snoring away; there's usually a couple of pairs of feet hanging from the end of the recliners,' he laughs.

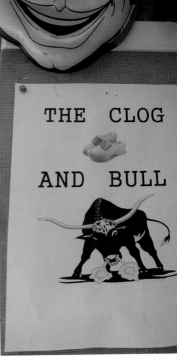

THE CLOG
AND BULL

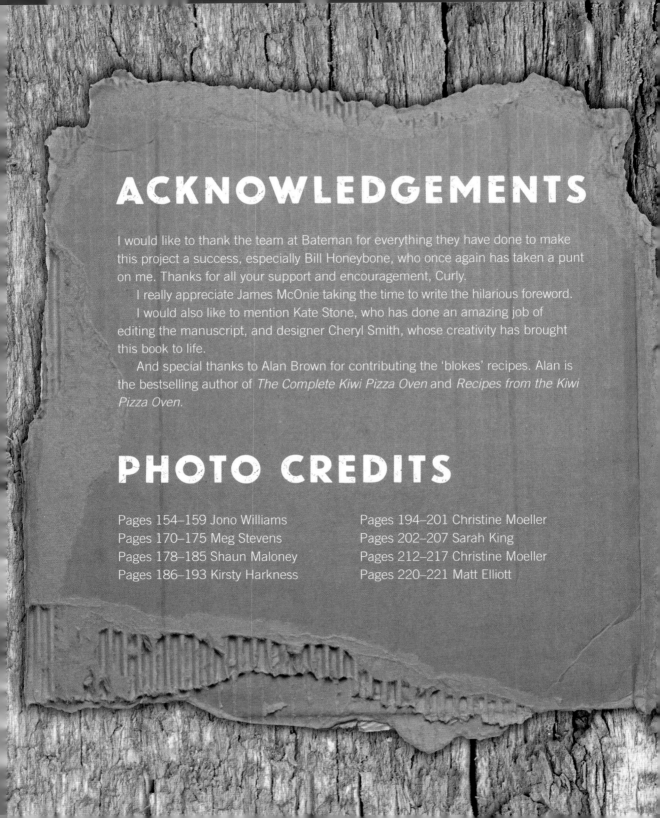

ACKNOWLEDGEMENTS

I would like to thank the team at Bateman for everything they have done to make this project a success, especially Bill Honeybone, who once again has taken a punt on me. Thanks for all your support and encouragement, Curly.

I really appreciate James McOnie taking the time to write the hilarious foreword.

I would also like to mention Kate Stone, who has done an amazing job of editing the manuscript, and designer Cheryl Smith, whose creativity has brought this book to life.

And special thanks to Alan Brown for contributing the 'blokes' recipes. Alan is the bestselling author of *The Complete Kiwi Pizza Oven* and *Recipes from the Kiwi Pizza Oven*.

PHOTO CREDITS

Pages 154–159 Jono Williams
Pages 170–175 Meg Stevens
Pages 178–185 Shaun Maloney
Pages 186–193 Kirsty Harkness

Pages 194–201 Christine Moeller
Pages 202–207 Sarah King
Pages 212–217 Christine Moeller
Pages 220–221 Matt Elliott